The $200 Silence

Everyone Might be Smiling, But Nobody's Okay

Rev. Dr. Ango Fomuso Ekellem

TechSyntar Publishing

TechSyntar M2Grow AfroGlobal

First Edition, December 2025.

ISBN: 978-1-970878-06-6

Dedication

To my mother, we call her Mere,
the silent power who reminds me that gentleness is strength.
You check in without being asked,
you notice the smallest things,
you give thanks for what others overlook,
and you never hold a grudge.
Your quiet consistency has been my greatest sermon.
You see beauty in the smallest corners of life,
and through your eyes I learned that love is not noise, it is
presence.

This book is also for every heart that reaches out,
for those who call just to ask, "How are you, really?"
for the ones who listen without fixing,
and for the quiet encouragers whose kindness holds others
together.

The $200 Silence exists for those who are tired of surface living.
For the leaders who can no longer watch their people suffer
behind smiles.
For the young professionals searching for meaning in endless
performance.
For the builders who feel misunderstood for caring too
much.

It is for the mothers juggling bills in silence,
for the fathers too proud to ask for help,
for the alumni who want more than dinner pictures,
and for the believers who know that faith must have hands.

It is a reminder that humanity still works.
That we can still build groups that are not toxic or
transactional.
That we can laugh and still be honest.
That love and structure can coexist.

It is also a challenge to stop waiting for others to fix the
brokenness.
We are the others.
The responsibility to rebuild belongs to every one of us who
sees the cracks.

Preface

The Show Must Go On... Until It Doesn't

You show up.
You smile.
You clap.
You contribute, sometimes.
You take the group photo.
You drop the laughing emoji.
You reply "Happy Birthday" or "RIP."
And you try not to be the one who brings the mood down.

Because that's what community looks like now, isn't it?

We say it's unity, but deep down we know: it's performance.

Underneath the events, the dinner outings, and the curated smiles, real people are hurting. Badly. But the pain doesn't fit the mood. It doesn't match the tone of the group. So the pain gets swallowed, silenced, tucked beneath pressed shirts and rehearsed laughter.

You watch people withdraw quietly. You see them skip events, go silent in the chat, disappear into the background. You notice they always have a reason they can't come. "Busy." "Next time." But deep down, you know what's happening.

They couldn't afford the ticket.

They didn't have transport.

They're barely surviving, and being part of the group is starting to feel like an impostor act. They don't belong, not because they don't care, but because they can't keep up. And in many spaces, that's unforgivable.

No one asks what's really going on. No one wonders who's caring for a sick parent, raising a child alone, skipping meals to pay rent, or silently slipping into depression. But when someone finally dies, suddenly or slowly, that's when the messages flood in.

"Gone too soon."
"He was such a good soul."
"Why didn't he say anything?"
"Let's show up for the funeral."

Suddenly, the same group that didn't have time to check in or grace to understand why he stopped paying dues becomes a sea of condolences and memorial photos. The tears arrive too late, and the questions they're asking now were the ones they should've asked while he was still alive.

This book is not about blaming. It's about naming what we've all felt but were too polite to say out loud.

There is a kind of community that looks beautiful but lacks substance.
There is a kind of togetherness that makes room for parties but not for pain.
There is a kind of friendship that celebrates your highs but misses your quiet cries.

But here's the truth. It doesn't take much to make it better. You don't need a committee or a campaign. Sometimes all it takes is:

- Paying attention to what someone isn't saying

- Noticing when a once-active friend has gone silent

- Asking the awkward question

- Privately offering a small bit of help, not as charity, but as dignity

- Saying, "You don't have to impress us. Just be here. We care."

Sometimes, it's just $200. Not for a loan. Not with interest. But because a mother needs to keep the lights on for her kids. Because someone is between jobs. Because someone just needs to breathe.

That small amount might be the difference between:

- Confidence and collapse

- A thank-you and a suicide note

- A return to community or a final disappearance

This book isn't only about survival. It's about prevention. About protecting one another before the collapse happens. Because funerals shouldn't be the place where we realize how much someone meant. They should be the place we celebrate a life that was supported, seen, and surrounded with love all along.

And so this book is for the ones who see.

The ones who notice the silence.
The ones who can't un-feel the gap between the birthday messages and the broken lives.
The ones who are tired of pretending that everything's okay when so much isn't.

The ones who long for something real. Something healing. Something holy.

You're not wrong for feeling it. You're not bitter. You're not dramatic.

You're just awake.

And this book is for you.

Let's build something that lasts.

Reflection

And so the question remains: what happens when silence becomes our survival strategy?

Contents

Fomuso Ekellem

Introduction: Now That the Party Is Over... What Next?

The Silence Between Celebrations

There is a rhythm to community life that feels comforting on the surface. The chatter in alumni groups, the photos from weekend gatherings, the laughter at reunions, the emojis flooding a birthday post. To the outside world, it looks like we've got it together, well-connected, successful, strong, unbreakable. But beneath that rhythm, a quieter melody hums, one few ever notice. It is the sound of people barely hanging on, whispering prayers no one hears.

In many circles, people are drowning quietly. Not in the dramatic, headline-making way, but in subtle, silent struggles that rarely earn attention. Someone has missed two months' rent and keeps smiling on the group video call. Another has an eviction notice folded beneath a Bible or stuffed inside a drawer. Someone else has sold their phone just to buy food for the week, but they still manage to comment "Beautiful!" under a photo of the group dinner they couldn't afford to attend.

You see, in modern communities, asking for help has become harder than suffering.

We tell each other to "be strong," to "trust God," to "hang in there," but we seldom create safe spaces where those words can become reality. For many, by the time anyone realizes something is wrong, the damage is done, the rent unpaid, the job gone, the spirit broken.

How do you even begin to say, *"I am not okay"* when everyone seems to be celebrating something? In a world that rewards confidence and polish, vulnerability feels like failure. People fear becoming "that person" who brings down the group's mood. They fear being whispered about, "He's struggling," "She's broke," "Things are not well." So they swallow their truth and perfect their smiles.

A woman named **Ngozi**, a mother of three from Port Harcourt, once shared how she stopped attending her old school alumni events. "Each time, it was one contribution after another," she said, her voice shaking between fatigue and pride. "Uniforms for the gala, tickets for dinner, donations for the building project. I wanted to be part of it, but my husband had lost his job. I couldn't contribute, so I stayed away." Months later, the group learned she had been evicted. No one had known. They sent words of comfort after the damage was irreversible.

The saddest part is that most people do not mean harm. They are not heartless; they are simply unaware. Communities often operate like stage plays. Everyone knows their lines, their cues, their costumes, but few look behind the curtain. In some circles, the motto is almost sacred: *"Suffer in private, celebrate in public."* Those words sound like strength, but they're poison.

And yet, they echo through spiritual gatherings too. "Withdraw and heal," they say. "Keep your battles to yourself." But isolation is not always healing; sometimes it's slow destruction. Sometimes a person doesn't need solitude; they need $200 to cover rent, or a phone call that says, "I noticed you've been quiet. Are you okay?" That small gesture can be the wall that keeps a life from collapsing.

I've watched it happen in my own circles. In Germany, I once belonged to a vibrant African community group. We gathered for national holidays, children's parties, and church anniversaries. There was food, color, laughter, music, everything that reminded us of home. Yet, behind those joyous reunions, people were battling unseen wars. A brother from Kenya, who used to dance with contagious energy, suddenly stopped attending. We later learned he had been working three jobs to send money home, and when he couldn't keep up, he was evicted from his flat. Nobody knew until he disappeared completely. Another friend, a nurse from Ghana, suffered burnout in silence. Her posts stayed cheerful until one day, she collapsed from exhaustion at work.

Our group, like many others, was built on good intentions. But good intentions are not enough. There was no structure for support, no system to check on those missing in action, no emergency fund, no circle of accountability. Just smiles, pictures, and a deep belief that "everyone is fine."

When I moved to the United States for my sabbatical, the contrasts hit even harder. Germany had been stable; systems worked, rules protected, society held together by order. But here, in this wide new landscape, I found myself starting from scratch, rebuilding a business, caring for my children, and adjusting to my mother's aging needs. Even with faith, experience, and friends, it was hard. There were days when silence pressed heavy.

And during those days, I realized something profound: the hardest thing we do as humans is learning to receive help. We are taught from childhood that strength means independence, that asking is weakness. In Africa, we even have proverbs that celebrate endurance and mock vulnerability. But true community requires both, the grace to give and the humility to receive. Without that balance, relationships turn into performances, not lifelines.

Think of **Chinedu**, a young man from Lagos who relocated to Canada for his master's degree. He joined his university's African student group with enthusiasm, attending every party and event. But when his father passed and tuition payments fell behind, he went silent. "I didn't know how to say I was struggling," he told me later. "Everybody was posting success stories, buying cars, traveling. How do you ask for help when everyone else looks like they're winning?" By the time anyone noticed, he had dropped out. Today, he works two jobs, still pretending he's finishing his degree. His friends think he's on a research break.

We are surrounded by **Chinedus**, **Ngozis**, and countless others hiding behind cheerful emojis. The tragedy is not just that people are in need; it's that they are invisible in their need.

What if we could see earlier? What if we learned to notice when someone's laughter becomes thinner, or their participation fades? What if our communities had the courage to talk about what truly matters, rent, jobs, mental health, family burdens, instead of just event themes and dress codes? What if we could create structures where no one has to choose between dignity and survival?

Imagine this:
An alumni group that collects small monthly contributions, not for parties, but for emergency support.
A network where mentors help younger members find jobs

or build small businesses.
A culture that values quiet empathy as much as public celebration.
A community that listens.

These are not complicated reforms. They are simple fixes, human fixes. But they require something we've forgotten how to practice: authentic care.

In many African cultures, the word for "community" is deeply spiritual. In Swahili, *ujamaa* means familyhood, not blood, but belonging. In the Igbo language, *umunna* carries the idea that we are extensions of one another. Yet, somehow, in the rush of modern life, we've turned community into a performance arena. We gather to outshine, not to outlove. We network, but we don't nurture.

Some say, "Let's just party our stress away." And there's truth in that, joy heals. Dancing together, sharing laughter, it all matters. But what if we also dealt with the stress itself, so that our joy could be genuine? What if our celebrations came from hearts at peace, not souls pretending to be fine?

Children are dropping out of school because their parents can't afford fees. Adult children remain stuck at home, unable to find direction because life has bruised their confidence. Couples pretend everything is fine at family gatherings while barely speaking at home. Parents borrow to keep appearances. And then we all meet again next month for another reunion, another group photo, another toast to "progress."

Something in us knows it's not real.

Yet, even in that awareness, hope remains. I've seen what happens when one brave soul breaks the silence. A message as simple as, "Friends, I need help," can awaken something sacred in others. Suddenly, the masks drop, and people start sharing their truths. "Me too," one says. "I've been struggling too." That honesty can birth healing that no event could ever create.

Learning to See, Learning to Heal

Sometimes healing begins not with a grand plan but with a quiet decision to notice. To pause long enough to sense what is unsaid. To read the tone of a message, the silence after a joke, the missing name in the attendance list. In many of our communities, what breaks people is not poverty itself but the loneliness of being unseen. The human soul can endure hardship if it knows someone cares. But when care is replaced by performance, people collapse long before they fall.

In African cities, we have a saying: *"You cannot dance well on an empty stomach."* It means joy needs a foundation. Yet many of our gatherings have become marathons of dancing over hunger. We clap, we pose, we post, we laugh. And afterward, we go home to dark rooms and overdue bills. The silence after the music can be deafening.

I remember one December back in Darmstadt, Germany, during our university days, a friend named Kemi hosted our old school reunion. The theme was "Rekindling the Spirit." She decorated beautifully, cooked mountains of food, and hired a DJ. But halfway through the night, I noticed her slipping into the kitchen repeatedly. Later, I learned that she had borrowed money to host the event, hoping it would lift her own spirits after losing her job months earlier. The photos from that night were stunning. Everyone smiled. Yet behind every smile was exhaustion. That was the night I began to understand how much pain we hide behind celebration.

When Asking Feels Impossible

One of the most paralyzing truths about community life is how hard it is to ask for help. In theory, we all say we're available, "Call me if you need anything." But those words often mean, "Please don't call unless it's convenient." And so, when real need arises, we hesitate. We convince ourselves others are too busy. We tell ourselves, "Everyone is struggling; why should my problem matter?"

I once sat with a man named **Joseph**, a tailor from Ghana living in Hamburg. He was weeks away from eviction and still paying group dues because he didn't want to look irresponsible. When I asked why he didn't speak up, he said, "If I tell them, they'll think I'm lazy. Everyone is hustling." Two months later, he was homeless. The group heard only after a church member found him sleeping in his shop. They helped eventually, but by then the humiliation had already sunk in.

It made me wonder how many Josephs walk among us, wearing fine clothes sewn by their own hands while everything inside is unraveling.

We've been conditioned to measure worth by appearance. In some spiritual circles, people even say suffering in silence proves faith. But silence is not always strength; sometimes it is despair dressed in religion. Healing begins when we learn to separate pride from dignity. Dignity allows honesty. Pride demands disguise.

The Fear of Being a Burden

There's another layer to this struggle, the fear of overwhelming others. Many people genuinely believe their pain will be too much for their friends. They have watched helpers burn out or gossipers weaponize vulnerability, and so they retreat. "I'll handle it myself," they say, even when they clearly cannot.

When I relocated to the United States, I met an older Kenyan woman, **Mama Ruth**, who became like an aunt to my family. She worked as a caregiver, sending money home to educate her grandchildren. One day I found her crying quietly in her car after church. Her landlord had given her notice to vacate because of unpaid rent. I asked why she hadn't told anyone. "I didn't want to be that woman who always needs something," she said. "I have helped so many people. Let me suffer small." That "small" suffering turned into hospitalization after weeks of stress and malnutrition.

We often celebrate the giver and forget that receivers are the lifeblood of giving. Without receivers, generosity cannot exist. The healthiest communities know that the roles must rotate. Today you give, tomorrow you may receive. It is not weakness; it is rhythm.

Why We Miss the Warning Signs

People rarely fall apart overnight. There are always clues, missed calls, excuses, shorter texts, unpaid contributions, quiet withdrawals. But we have trained ourselves not to see. We tell ourselves everyone is fine because it is easier than facing the discomfort of empathy. Empathy demands time. It interrupts our plans. It asks for action.

A young man named **Tunde** from Ibadan once told me, "In my group chat, if you announce a wedding, you get 300 comments. If you post that you lost your job, maybe five people reply, and even they say, 'It is well.'" He laughed sadly, then added, "That's why I stopped sharing." This selective attention is the disease of modern connection, we react to excitement, not to emotion. We celebrate joy loudly and tiptoe around pain.

When we finally do gather for funerals, the shock is genuine. We cry, we post, we say, "If only we had known." But often we did know. We just didn't want to deal with what we knew. Death forces honesty in ways life does not. The question "What really happened?" becomes a mirror held too late.

The Myth of Endless Strength

In many African homes, children grow up hearing, "Be strong. Don't cry. Others have it worse." We wear that sentence like armor into adulthood. It helps us survive but keeps us from being real. Some even mistake exhaustion for faith, believing that perseverance without rest proves devotion.

But strength that refuses support is simply denial in disguise. True resilience allows help. It accepts that even warriors need water, that even prophets needed companions. Every strong person you admire has been held up by someone unseen. The tragedy is that in our current systems, those unseen hands are disappearing.

Imagine if, instead of waiting for breakdowns, we had check-in systems. Imagine every alumni group, church fellowship, or social club assigning three people to quietly monitor wellbeing, one handles professional connections, one looks out for welfare, one for emotional support. Imagine small funds for emergencies, created not from guilt but from foresight. Such structures turn empathy into policy. They make kindness sustainable.

When Joy Becomes Real

I once attended a wedding where the couple did something remarkable. Instead of the usual expensive decor, they asked guests to contribute toward a community education fund. During the ceremony, they invited two single mothers whose children had benefited from that fund to speak. The entire hall was in tears. The celebration still had music and dancing, but it felt different. It was joy rooted in purpose. That night, I realized what genuine celebration feels like, not escape from pain but victory over it.

What if our communities learned that same principle? What if every event left behind something lasting, a scholarship, a mentorship pairing, a medical bill paid, a small loan granted? We could still dance, still laugh, still shine. But the shine would heal.

The African Thread of Togetherness

Long before hashtags and alumni platforms, African societies survived through extended kinship. Villages shared harvests. Neighbors raised children together. Families contributed to each other's weddings and funerals without being asked. The line between "mine" and "ours" was blurred by love. Somewhere along modernization, that thread loosened. Migration, urban life, and digital living replaced presence with performance. Yet, the essence of *ubuntu*, "I am because we are," still whispers beneath the noise. We can bring it back, but it requires humility. It requires slowing down enough to see beyond the screens.

I have seen glimpses of it return. In Atlanta, I met a group of African women who created a "Transition Table." Each month, members placed $20 into a shared purse. When one person faced a crisis, a car repair, a sick child, a missed rent, the table responded quietly. No public announcements, no drama. Just compassion made practical. Within a year, their unity became a testimony that spread to other cities.

Healing does not require perfection. It requires intentionality. It means deciding that people matter more than appearances. It means replacing the phrase "Let's just meet" with "Let's make meaning."

My Own Mirror

When I left Germany to care for my mother and rebuild my life, I understood firsthand how transitions humble us. I had stability there, friends, predictable systems. Starting over in the United States was daunting. There were mornings I questioned everything, the move, the timing, even my calling. Yet those same moments became the soil where this book grew. Every phone call from a friend who checked in, every message that said "How are you holding up?" felt like oxygen. I learned that simple attention is sacred.

This project was born from that realization, that attention saves lives. That noticing is ministry. That you don't have to be rich to rescue; sometimes all it takes is empathy wrapped in action. I want every reader to see themselves not only as potential givers but also as deserving receivers. Because no matter how capable you are, life eventually brings a season where you need someone to hold your arms up.

The New Way Forward

If communities are to survive, we must rebuild from the inside out. Start with honesty. Make check-ins normal. Celebrate transparency as strength. Encourage both giving and receiving. Replace judgment with curiosity, "How are you really?" Learn to listen without rushing to fix. And when fixing is needed, act quietly but effectively.

Our gatherings should reflect both joy and justice. Our friendships should hold both laughter and accountability. Our online groups should move beyond emojis into genuine connection. The world doesn't need more events; it needs more empathy.

When the Music Stops

So, now that the party is over, what next? Do we simply wait for the next one, pretending again that everything is fine? Or do we finally pause, breathe, and rebuild something lasting?

Real community begins the moment we decide to replace spectacle with substance. It begins when we see each other not as competitors in success but as co-laborers in survival and growth. It begins when $200 becomes more than money; it becomes a message: *You are not alone.*

I believe we can return to that kind of humanity. It won't happen in one meeting or one book, but it can start here, with us, right now. Because in the end, the goal is simple.

Let's build communities where no one has to suffer silently, where help is not an afterthought, and where joy is genuine because every soul is seen.

That is the heart of *The $200 Silence.*

And if we can master that art, of seeing, caring, and giving space for both strength and weakness, then maybe, just maybe, the next time we dance, it will be because peace has finally joined the celebration.

Reflection

I thought I was fine, until I realized I had mastered survival more than living.

Everyone Might be Smiling, But Nobody's Okay

Chapter 1: The $200 Silence

The Performance of Survival

I played the game well, perhaps too well. The game of showing up, smiling, and keeping everything looking intact while the roof overhead quietly trembled. It is a performance many of us perfect: appearing composed, capable, and in control while holding chaos together with sheer will. In many African settings, silence is often misread as pride. When someone withdraws, we assume dignity, strategy, or emotional distance. We rarely suspect exhaustion, loneliness, or the slow erosion that comes from surviving for too long without rest. In my case, that withdrawal and silence were not pride. They were tiredness. They were confusion.

I encouraged conversations in groups, gathered professionals so we could grow together and expose our children to what was possible. I showcased the work of others without diminishing my own, sharing my finished projects because I believed balance mattered. I celebrated those who were rising, encouraged freely, and pressed for AI integration, for awareness of the fast-approaching era, for learning data, collecting it properly, and conducting real research. But the soil was not ready, and I felt myself slowly burning out. I was blunt at times, because clarity felt necessary. Meanwhile, during my sabbatical in the United States, I sat before a computer for ten hours a day, trying to keep my work alive, writing grants, meeting potential clients who wanted endless conversation but delayed registration payments, answering questions that rarely became contracts, and quietly wondering how the next rent would be paid.

There's a strange irony to it. I serve people daily, solving their problems, improving their lives through my work, yet living with the quiet fear that I might lose my own home. When clients delay payment or ask for discounts, they rarely picture the person behind the screen juggling invoices and bills, hoping one project closes before another collapses. We live in a society that applauds productivity but ignores fragility.

When I fell behind on rent, I convinced myself it was temporary. It always is, until it isn't. My landlord had been polite, firm, and predictable. But when the lease renewal came up, his tone changed. He suddenly wanted to sell the house, or so he said. It wasn't clear at first. I suspected it had more to do with my late payments. Still, I held my peace. Then a family member, well-meaning and blunt, said, "Keep the last rent. Tell him your deposit will cover it since you're moving." I obeyed. It seemed practical at the time.

That decision was actually the best since to led to the ultimate lease extension, yet it opened a new chapter of anxiety the during the next few days. The landlord, perhaps provoked by the act, revealed that he had not planned to sell. He had only hesitated to renew because of my previous delays. He then asked for a new lease, but with conditions: double deposit and two months' rent upfront. It was not hostility; it was protection. For him, it was business. For me, it was survival.

For two weeks, I negotiated, prayed, emailed, explained, and swallowed pride. In the end, we settled on a normal extension. But those two weeks drained me more than ten years of ministry ever had. I was not angry with him. I was simply humanly tired.

The entire episode revealed something deeper about community, culture, and silence. It showed how, even when we live among people, we often live alone. Everyone around me was busy fighting their own battles, hustling to meet their own needs. Nobody noticed that I was drifting, that I was juggling invoices by day and uncertainty by night. In the African immigrant community, people see you working and assume you're fine. You're posting online, smiling with your children, replying to messages, so you must be doing well. That's the myth.

But behind those smiles are invisible rents, unrenewed contracts, children's school fees, car repairs, and sometimes just pure emotional fatigue. Yet we keep playing the game because in our world, to admit struggle feels like shame.

It doesn't help that our own people often create invisible hierarchies of respect. The quieter you are, the more people assume you are powerful or wise. The more scarce your presence, the more they assume you are "making moves." So we reward absence and mistake it for achievement. Meanwhile, some of those "absent" people are not strategizing; they are breaking.

In African cultures, silence used to be sacred. It meant thoughtfulness, restraint, maturity. But in this new age, it has become camouflage. We don't know anymore who is being wise and who is being crushed. We clap for performances, not for endurance.

When I think back on those rent struggles, I remember the irony of watching Africans pay promptly to foreign companies while negotiating endlessly with their own. It is not wickedness; it is habit. Many of us carry a colonial shadow in our subconscious. We respect what is distant and devalue what is familiar. We postpone payments to our brothers and sisters but wire money immediately to strangers. We forget that the delay we call "negotiation" might be someone's last thread of stability.

The emotional cost of that behavior is immense. It creates communities where trust thins out and empathy fades. Everyone begins to perform strength because weakness attracts debtors or gossip. Nobody admits they are behind. Everyone owes someone something, financially or emotionally. The culture of performance becomes armor, but that armor also suffocates.

I remember one evening when my children were watching cartoons, and I sat by the window pretending to read. In truth, I was praying silently, asking God for wisdom and for clients who paid on time. I felt embarrassed that simple rent had become such a mountain. Yet part of me knew it was not just about the money. It was about the exhaustion of constantly being "fine."

The calls kept coming. Clients wanted revisions, explanations, ideas. They wanted excellence, speed, and creativity. Some asked for discounts because "business is slow." And I kept delivering, smiling through every call, thanking them for the opportunity. I never mentioned that I was running out of food or that my landlord had just asked for a double deposit. To them, I was a reliable professional. To myself, I was a woman

18

holding together two worlds, the visible and the invisible. A woman relearning the renting game after nearly two decades of home ownership in her country of origin, now navigating a brand-new nation with unfamiliar laws, far from home, and expected to adapt without faltering. We tell ourselves this is adulthood. But sometimes it is simply isolation wearing a business suit.

The Illusion of Strength

Many Africans abroad live inside this same illusion. We see each other at gatherings and pretend we're all thriving. We laugh about politics, about the exchange rate, about our home countries, but we avoid the real question: "How are you surviving, really?" It's not malice. It's discomfort. Vulnerability feels like exposure.

And so, we build friendships based on humor, not honesty. We meet, eat, take photos, and return home carrying the same burdens we arrived with. The next morning, we scroll through photos from the night before and comment "Good vibes only," even though half the people in the picture went home to unpaid bills.

I have seen people use humor as a shield. They will joke about being broke while smiling, but if you listen closely, you will hear despair woven into the laughter. It takes courage to look beyond the joke and ask, "Do you need help?" That question is powerful. But it is rarely asked.

In our culture, independence is a badge of honor. But independence can also become isolation. We forget that even strong people need softness, even leaders need listeners. When we assume everyone is fine, we rob them of the chance to be real.

This is why I called it *The $200 Silence*. Because sometimes, all someone needs is that little support, that little check-in, that small loan, or just a sincere question. It's not about the amount. It's about awareness. The silence is not golden anymore; it is dangerous.

The Hidden Currents of Entitlement

Another layer to this crisis lies in our unspoken expectations. Many Africans believe that because we share culture, faith, or continent, we owe each other understanding by default. That assumption breeds disappointment. We expect empathy without communication. We assume others will "get it," but they don't. Everyone interprets silence differently.

Some think you are too proud to ask. Some think you are too busy to care. Others think you are too successful to need anything. Miscommunication grows like weeds. Soon, the same people you hope will help you start whispering that you've changed. They don't know you are simply fighting invisible fires.

Entitlement also shows up in business. I have had clients who insisted on discounts because we share African roots. "Ah, sister, do it small for me now," they say. Yet these same people will pay full price elsewhere. It's not cruelty; it's a mindset. Familiarity makes people forget your labor. They assume your effort is flexible because your relationship is close.

What they don't see is that every discount they request, every delayed payment they justify, chips away at the builder's spirit.

It's not the money alone; it's the message that your work deserves less. When that message repeats long enough, it becomes internalized. You start to feel invisible.

There's an old African proverb that says, "A tree that bears fruit must endure many stones." But in today's world, the stones come not only from enemies but from friends who do not understand the cost of your fruit.

So we continue performing. We wear strength like perfume. We say, "All is well," even when it's not. And slowly, the gap between who we are and who we appear to be widens. That gap is the silence.

I wish I could say I stopped playing the game after my rent ordeal, but the truth is, performance is addictive. It gives momentary dignity. It lets you breathe in a world that values appearance more than authenticity. But every performance extracts a price. The exhaustion builds until one day, even pretending becomes too heavy.

That is where many people are right now, smiling on the outside, crumbling on the inside, waiting for someone to notice.

The Price of Pretending

When I look back on that season, what stands out is not the difficulty itself but the strange calm that came with pretending. Pretending is exhausting, but it also creates a kind of temporary comfort. You convince yourself that if you keep smiling long enough, the pain will somehow dissolve. You hope the bills will sort themselves out, that the delayed clients will pay, that the landlord will suddenly call with kindness in his voice. You keep acting strong because everyone expects you to be.

Pretending becomes a way to survive embarrassment. In a culture where people rarely separate struggle from shame, admitting need feels like confessing sin. You smile, attend the next event, post the right photo, and keep moving. And yet, somewhere between the smiles and the silence, your energy begins to leak.

I saw it in myself. I could feel the weight in my chest every morning. The more I tried to hold it all together, the more it felt like I was fading. Not physically, but emotionally. I woke up tired, prayed distractedly, and worked longer hours just to silence the inner noise. It is one thing to be broke; it is another to be broken quietly.

One night, as I sat in front of my computer after another day of unpaid hours, I remembered the words of an old friend from Lagos who used to say, "Africa is full of people pretending to be fine for people pretending to care." It sounded harsh back then, but in that moment, I understood. The world had turned into a stage where we clap for each other's pain as long as it is beautifully presented.

We call it resilience, but sometimes it's just suppression.

When Silence is Misread

In the African setting, silence is complicated. If you speak too much, you are called talkative. If you go quiet, you are called proud. If you appear too calm, people assume you are doing well. If you look worried, they say you lack faith. And so, many of us hide between those labels, never quite understood, never truly free.

There was a brother in our community group named **Patrick**, a sharp-minded engineer who used to contribute passionately to discussions. One day, his messages stopped. When he finally reappeared, he wrote a long post full of impressive words and philosophy. Everyone applauded his "wisdom." They didn't realize he was slipping into depression. His long silence wasn't strategy; it was sorrow. His big words were camouflage.

It's easy to mistake eloquence for stability. We assume that people who speak well are doing well. We assume that silence means self-control. But sometimes, silence is what people do when they are tired of explaining themselves.

In my own circle, I noticed how easy it was to celebrate performance. If you post success, the world gathers to cheer you. But if you share struggle, people disappear quietly. Struggle makes others uncomfortable because it mirrors their own hidden fears. So we scroll past, tell ourselves, "He will be fine," and move on.

This habit has made us a generation of observers, not participants. We witness each other's pain from a safe distance. We talk about community, but we practice avoidance.

Why Empathy Costs Energy

Empathy is tiring work. It demands you step outside your own storm to help someone else navigate theirs. It takes time, sensitivity, and often money. For people already in survival mode, empathy feels like an extra burden. That is why communities struggle to care deeply. Everyone is fighting their own fires.

But this is where faith and maturity must step in. If we only help when it's convenient, we will always be surrounded by unseen suffering. Real community is not built on convenience; it is built on conviction.

I learned this again when a client from Nigeria, a mother of four, confided that she was about to lose her shop. Her voice trembled when she said, "I don't even need a miracle. I just need a pause." That sentence struck me. A pause. That's what most people need. Not a massive rescue, not a miracle, just a moment of relief, a small window of grace to breathe. Sometimes that pause costs only $200. But silence makes it unreachable.

When Help Feels Risky

There is another side to the silence. It is not just about those who need help; it is also about those afraid to give it. People hesitate to help because they fear being taken advantage of. We have seen generosity abused. We have seen borrowed money vanish with friendship. We have seen people pretend to be victims to gain sympathy. All these experiences have made us suspicious, even cynical.

So we wait for undeniable proof of suffering before we act. But by the time the proof appears, it is often too late. Someone has already been evicted, or humiliated, or lost hope.

In Germany, a friend once told me how his church started a "Silent Aid Fund." They collected small anonymous donations and used them to help members quietly when they noticed signs of struggle. No one had to beg. No one had to explain. It worked beautifully until one person misused the fund. The trust broke, and the fund collapsed. But what struck me was that even with the failure, many said it had been the most compassionate initiative their church ever attempted. That tells you how hungry people are for quiet, dignified help.

The Fatigue of Strength

There comes a point when you get tired of being strong. You reach a place where even encouragement feels heavy. You listen to motivational talks, read affirmations, and still feel empty. It is not that you lack faith; it is that you have been running on fumes for too long.

I remember one evening when my children were asleep, and I sat on the couch staring at the ceiling. The rent issue had finally been resolved, but the exhaustion lingered. I realized I had been living in a constant state of alertness, like a soldier waiting for another battle. That is what survival does. It keeps you sharp but drains your soul.

I whispered a prayer that night, not for money, not for success, but for rest. Not physical rest, but emotional rest. The kind that allows you to be honest without fear of judgment.

The Invisible Battle

Behind every confident African abroad, there is a story the world does not see. We look polished because we must be. We cannot afford to appear weak in countries that already question our worth. We work twice as hard to be seen as equal, and we fear that any sign of struggle will confirm someone's prejudice.

So, we fight invisible battles. We send money home while living on borrowed time. We help relatives, sponsor siblings, contribute to funerals, and still smile. It's not pride; it's pressure. And when the pressure breaks someone, we act shocked.

I once met a young man in Dallas who had everything going for him, or so it seemed. He drove a good car, dressed well, and was always cheerful. One day, his friend called me in tears. The man had taken his life. Later we learned he had been battling debt for months. He told no one. Everyone thought he was fine.

We have become experts at looking fine.

The Small Fixes That Save Lives

The solution is not complicated. We need to return to the simple art of noticing. When someone goes quiet, check in. When a friend declines an invitation repeatedly, ask why. When a colleague looks distracted, care enough to ask what's wrong.

We also need practical systems of support. Imagine if every social group created a small emergency fund for members. Nothing dramatic, just a pool of kindness. Imagine if we normalized asking for help without shame, and if we stopped attaching spiritual failure to financial struggle.

One of the best lessons I learned came from a woman in Atlanta who runs a small African grocery store. She told me, "I don't give people money, but I let them buy food on credit. When they pay, fine. If they don't, I count it as my charity." That philosophy changed me. She understood that compassion can be structured. You don't have to be rich to care; you just need to be intentional.

When We Begin to Heal

Healing starts when we stop performing and start connecting. It begins with honesty. You cannot heal what you keep hiding. We must learn to replace pride with presence. To say, "I'm not okay today," and trust that our community will not see it as weakness but as truth.

It also requires us to see others clearly. Sometimes the most successful-looking person in the room is the most exhausted. Sometimes the loudest laughter hides the deepest ache. True friendship means listening beyond words.

The miracle of compassion is that it heals both the giver and the receiver. When you reach out, you feel human again. When you are helped, you feel seen again. Both are sacred experiences.

My Quiet Lesson

As I look back on that difficult period of my life, I realize it taught me how to see people differently. I no longer measure anyone by their appearance or their posts. I now ask quieter questions. I listen to the pauses between words.

My landlord and I eventually found peace. The house remained, the children settled, and life moved on. But something inside me changed permanently. I began to understand that strength is not the absence of struggle. It is the decision to keep loving, giving, and showing up even when life feels unfair.

That season taught me that the silence we fear breaking is often the bridge to our healing.

The Truth Beneath the Smiles

Every photo we take hides a truth. Every laughter-filled gathering carries its share of unspoken battles. But that does not make joy fake. It makes it precious. Joy becomes authentic when it coexists with honesty. We can dance and still be real. We can celebrate and still care.

When I finally exhaled after the storm, I realized the goal is not to eliminate struggle but to make sure no one faces it alone. If this book accomplishes anything, I hope it reminds people that help is not pity and silence is not strength.

Some days, I still catch myself playing the old game, pretending, smiling, performing. Then I remember the lesson of that season and whisper to myself, "You don't have to play anymore."

Because healing begins the moment we tell the truth.

Reflection

When survival becomes performance, the next act is usually a photo proof that we are still standing.

Chapter 2: When Photos Replace Purpose

The Price of Applause

In many African communities, worth is often measured not by wisdom, but by the weight of your wallet. The moment someone drops a large contribution at a community event, the atmosphere changes. Eyes turn, voices soften, chairs shift to make space. If a man pledges one thousand dollars toward a cause, his opinions suddenly carry more authority. People begin to quote him, laugh louder at his jokes, and listen more intently when he speaks.

At least, until the next contribution.

Respect has become temporary, purchased, and recycled. It lasts only as long as your generosity performs. When the next event comes and another donor outshines you, the spotlight moves on. It is a cycle of applause that feeds the ego but starves the soul.

It is not that giving is bad. Giving is beautiful. But when contribution becomes the only language of influence, community loses its heart. True respect cannot be bought; it is earned through integrity and compassion. Yet in too many African circles, generosity is not seen as service but as a strategy, a way to gain attention and be seen as important.

There was a meeting I once attended where the emcee called out the names of contributors. Each name came with claps and praise. "Our brother, one thousand dollars!" The crowd erupted. "Our sister, five hundred!" More cheers. When it got to those who gave less, the applause softened. Some even whispered, "Ah, that's all she could do?"

I sat quietly, watching how human value was being measured in real time. The louder the claps, the greater the influence. The smaller the donation, the smaller the voice. And yet, behind many of those generous hands were quiet hearts in pain.

Some of the loudest givers are the loneliest people in the room. They donate not from abundance but from a desperate need to be seen. They want to matter, to belong, to silence the whisper that says, "You're not enough." So they give until it hurts, and when the applause fades, the emptiness returns.

The Hidden Ache of Generosity

I have met people who contribute heavily to community projects yet go home to unpaid bills. They smile in public but cry in private. Their giving is not a sign of wealth; it is a disguise for pain. They fear that if they stop giving, they will also stop being valued.

There was a man I knew, a successful-looking entrepreneur from Abuja, always impeccably dressed, always the first to pledge at meetings. He gave so much that everyone called him "the pillar." One day, I found him sitting alone in his car after an event. He looked tired. He told me quietly, "I give because when I stop, they forget me." That sentence never left me.

Many Africans are caught in this performance, a cycle of visible generosity and invisible suffering. They are respected for their giving but never helped for their needs. Because once you are labeled "the strong one," the world stops checking on you.

And the cycle deepens.

These are the people who need therapy, rest, or just one honest conversation. But they maintain the facade. To ask for help would ruin the image they have built. So they keep performing until they break.

When Generosity Masks Pain

There is an unspoken hierarchy in our communities: those who give money, those who talk, and those who listen. Someone made a condescending statement to me, and my sister said something like, "Have you started paying any money there?" She said I should stay quiet until I made some financial contributions. That stayed with me for a while. That was not meant to hurt but was given as genuine cultural advice, one that I despise wholly. But there is a long way to go before that is truly corrected. At first, I laughed, but later, the weight of that statement sank in. How did our minds become so commercialized that voices are priced by cash flow?

It is a dangerous conditioning, the idea that money equals wisdom and poverty equals silence. When communities operate on that rule, they silence some of their best minds. Those with fewer resources often carry the deepest insights, but they remain quiet because they feel unworthy to speak.

Money talks loudly, but truth speaks quietly. And too often, truth goes unheard.

The problem is not giving. The problem is how we reward it. We have made giving transactional, not transformational. Contributions now buy influence, titles, and even spiritual validation. Some people's prayers are valued more simply because they come with a check. We have confused generosity with godliness.

This culture creates impostors, people who act successful to maintain respect, even when they are falling apart. It creates a parade of broken hearts dressed in designer clothes, driving luxury cars but crying on the steering wheel.

I once attended a charity dinner where a young woman in a red dress gave a donation that drew gasps from the crowd. Later, in the restroom, I overheard her on the phone pleading with her landlord for an extension. Her voice trembled as she said, "I just need one more week." I stood frozen, realizing how deeply we misread people.

The Optics of Success

Social media has intensified this tragedy. It has turned the performance of wealth into a daily ritual. We post, we flaunt, we filter, we perform. We curate our lives like exhibitions. Even our pain must look poetic.

People now plan their posts more carefully than their prayers. A person could be hungry and still post a photo from a restaurant they cannot afford, just to maintain a reputation. It is not vanity; it is survival in a culture where image equals opportunity.

But optics come with a cost. Every time we pretend, we teach others to do the same. We create a chain of envy, comparison, and quiet despair. Those watching think everyone else is thriving, so they hide their own pain. The result is a society full of smiling faces and broken hearts.

We used to gather to share burdens. Now we gather to share photos. We used to build relationships around empathy; now we build them around impressions. We used to tell stories that healed; now we tell stories that sell.

When Reality Feels Like Failure

For many Africans abroad, the pressure to appear successful is crushing. We feel accountable not only to our families but to an entire community back home that measures worth by evidence of progress. Every visit home must look like triumph. Every photo must confirm that "abroad" is working. So we stretch ourselves to maintain the illusion, even when the reality is heavy.

I remember visiting a friend who had just moved to the U.S. She lived in a small apartment, but on social media, she looked like a celebrity. She posted photos from borrowed cars, fancy cafes, and smiling selfies with captions like "Thankful for the blessings." When I visited her in person, she confessed that she sometimes cried at night because she couldn't send money home. But she said, "If they know how hard it is, they will stop respecting me."

That sentence reveals a painful truth: in many African communities, pain disqualifies you. You are not allowed to struggle publicly. You must always appear strong, composed, and blessed.

This constant performance destroys authenticity. It robs us of real friendship. Because friendship cannot thrive in an atmosphere of pretending.

The Comparison Trap

The culture of optics thrives on comparison. We scroll through photos, compare our lives, and measure our happiness against someone else's highlight reel. The competition is silent but exhausting.

I once heard someone say, "In Africa, success is when your neighbor envies you." That mindset is poison. It keeps us chasing validation instead of purpose. It makes us celebrate envy instead of empathy.

And so, we buy what we can't afford, pledge what we can't sustain, and smile when we want to scream. Because the worst sin in our culture is to look like you're failing.

The Social Media Mirage

Technology has connected us but disconnected our souls. A person can have thousands of followers and still have no one to call when life falls apart. Likes have replaced listening. Comments have replaced conversation. We are together online but alone in real life.

And yet, deep down, people crave authenticity. They want to see real stories, real emotions, real struggles. They want to know they're not the only ones hurting. But the fear of being judged keeps everyone performing.

The saddest part is how the culture of performance has infected even our spiritual spaces. Churches, associations, and cultural groups sometimes prioritize appearances over compassion. The one who dresses well and gives loudly is respected. The one who sits quietly and weeps silently is ignored.

This is not who we are meant to be.

We come from traditions of community, where people shared meals, not masks. Where neighbors noticed when someone's child was missing from school. Where elders spoke value into the poor and wisdom into the young. Somewhere along the line, we traded that for status updates and sponsorship packages.

We replaced connection with competition.

And the result is exhaustion.

Restoring Purpose Over Performance

We live in an age where people would rather appear kind than actually be kind. It is easier to post sympathy than to practice it. Easier to share a hashtag than to show up. Easier to type "sending prayers" than to truly pray. The digital world has created a strange illusion of intimacy, a performance of compassion that demands no real sacrifice.

But the truth is, you cannot fake empathy for long. At some point, the emptiness catches up. The same photos we use to prove we are happy start to mock us. The likes fade quickly, and the silence after the applause feels louder than before. That is when many realize that validation is not connection.

I have often wondered what would happen if we could turn all that energy we spend on appearances into genuine community. If the time we use for posting was used for visiting someone who is struggling, how different would our lives look? What if every comment of "Congratulations!" was followed by a private message that said, "How are you holding up, really?"

True community is not built on optics. It is built on observation, on paying attention to the small details that reveal the truth behind the image.

Learning to See Again

Some time ago, I met a woman named **Efe** at a networking event in Houston. She was radiant, confident, and full of laughter. Everyone seemed drawn to her. Later, during a quiet moment, she told me she had just finalized her divorce but hadn't told anyone. "If they know," she said, "they will look at me differently. So I keep smiling."

Her confession pierced me. It reminded me that behind every vibrant photo, there may be a storm. Many Africans abroad carry silent wars behind polished smiles. The problem is that our communities are not structured to detect quiet pain. We are trained to notice success, not sorrow.

If someone buys a new car, everyone notices. But if that same person grows quieter each week, no one asks why. We assume silence means peace. Yet silence can mean struggle.

Relearning how to see is an act of love. It means noticing beyond the surface, hearing what people do not say, reading between their smiles. It means refusing to be fooled by filters and fancy captions.

I remember visiting a friend in Maryland whose social media feed looked like a dream. When I arrived, her fridge was empty. She laughed it off, saying, "I've been meaning to shop." Later she admitted she had been out of work for months. "I can't tell anyone," she said. "They will gossip." That fear is killing our communities. When vulnerability becomes a liability, everyone starts pretending.

We need to reclaim honesty as strength.

The False God of Status

Status has become our new religion. We worship it through possessions, through curated lives, through constant competition. In many gatherings, people introduce themselves not by who they are but by what they own or where they work. We compete for admiration like it is oxygen.

But status is a fragile god. It demands continuous sacrifice. You must keep proving yourself to stay relevant. You must outshine yesterday's version of yourself. You must never let the world see you sweat.

This endless striving creates exhaustion and envy. We begin to see life as a contest instead of a gift. We stop rejoicing for others because their joy reminds us of our own frustration. And when we cannot compete, we withdraw, convinced that our quiet seasons mean failure.

Yet some of the most meaningful lives are built in obscurity. Some of the strongest people are those who have nothing to prove. Their peace does not come from applause but from alignment. They do not need to flash anything to feel valuable.

There was an elderly man in our church who always dressed simply and sat quietly in the back row. People often overlooked him. Later I discovered that he paid the rent for two struggling families in secret. He never wanted public thanks. "I don't want to take God's glory," he said. That kind of humility is rare now. We crave recognition more than righteousness.

When Purpose Replaces Performance

Restoring purpose means remembering why we gather in the first place. The goal of community is not to impress but to impact. We were never meant to compete for attention; we were meant to complement one another's strengths.

In the old African village, every person had value. The hunter, the storyteller, the weaver, the midwife — all were essential. No one had to prove their worth through grand gestures. Each contribution, however small, was part of the whole. But today, value is assigned by visibility. If people can't see what you do, they assume you do nothing.

We must return to the wisdom of substance over show. A community thrives not when everyone shines alone, but when everyone stands together. The richest among us should not only give money but also mentor. The skilled should teach. The strong should protect. The compassionate should comfort. That is how purpose replaces performance.

When people are seen for who they are, not just for what they can give, healing begins.

The Taboo of Mental Health

Another reality we avoid discussing is mental health. In many African circles, emotional pain is still treated as weakness or spiritual failure. Depression is explained away as laziness. Anxiety is dismissed as lack of faith. People suffer quietly, terrified of being misunderstood.

I once counseled a young man who told me, "I'd rather people think I'm broke than think I'm depressed." His words reveal a deep stigma. We would rather confess financial struggle than emotional struggle. Yet many of the financial crises we see are rooted in mental fatigue, burnout, anxiety, hopelessness.

We must learn that seeking therapy is not betrayal of faith. It is stewardship of life. Healing the mind honors the God who gave it. When people can say, "I need help," without fear of ridicule, our communities will finally grow healthy again.

The Courage to Ask

One of the hardest things to do is to ask for help. Not because help is unavailable, but because pride is a heavy burden. Many of us fear that asking will shrink our image. But there is nothing noble about silent suffering.

We must normalize need. We must make it safe to say, "I'm struggling," without losing dignity. This requires empathy, not pity. Empathy listens; pity looks down.

Help is not always financial. Sometimes it is time, mentorship, encouragement, or simple presence. Sometimes all someone needs is to know they are not invisible. I have seen lives saved by a timely phone call, a meal shared, a word spoken with care.

One day, after I preached at a small community meeting, a woman approached me in tears. She said, "I don't even need money. I just needed someone to notice me." That sentence reminded me that the most powerful form of generosity is attention.

Reclaiming Real Connection

Rebuilding authentic community begins with small, consistent acts of sincerity.

When someone shares a success, celebrate without envy. When someone confides a struggle, protect their story. When someone disappears from the group, check in quietly. When you see someone always giving, ask if they need rest. When you notice someone always smiling, look into their eyes; you may see the truth hiding there.

Communities heal when we replace judgment with curiosity, gossip with grace, and performance with presence.

It is time to make relationships sacred again. Not transactional, not strategic, but spiritual; a space where people can breathe without pretending.

From Photos to Purpose

The title of this chapter, *When Photos Replace Purpose*, is not a condemnation of joy or celebration. It is a reminder that pictures should tell stories of real life, not hide them. Let our photos show laughter, yes, but also learning. Let them show growth, not just glamour. Let them record the meals shared with the lonely, the kindness extended to the struggling, the quiet moments of gratitude that never trend online.

Photos fade, but purpose endures.

Our children need to see that purpose-driven lives bring more fulfillment than applause-driven ones. They need to grow up understanding that self-worth is not found in brand names, cars, or followers, but in the depth of one's integrity and compassion.

The Call to Authenticity

If we want to heal our communities, we must unlearn the art of performing. We must dare to be seen as human again. That means showing up with our imperfections, our scars, and our lessons. It means telling the truth, even when the truth is messy.

We cannot keep building societies where value depends on spectacle. The world does not need more polished people; it needs honest ones.

When you drop the act, you invite others to do the same. When you speak honestly, you give permission for authenticity. That is how revival begins, not in events or applause, but in quiet hearts deciding to live truthfully.

A New Kind of Wealth

The wealth we must begin to pursue is not financial alone. It is the wealth of community, of peace, of mental stability, of mutual respect. True prosperity is collective. It grows when we lift one another, not when we outshine one another.

If we could learn to celebrate humility as much as we celebrate wealth, to honor consistency as much as charisma, and to respect sincerity as much as style, our gatherings would become healing spaces again.

The richest communities are not those with the biggest donors, but those with the biggest hearts.

When Purpose Shines Again

At the end of it all, the noise of performance fades. The applause quiets. The photos lose their glow. But what remains is the impact we made on real lives. That is the true legacy.

Purpose does not seek attention; it seeks meaning. It builds people, not impressions. It restores dignity instead of demanding it.

As I write this, I think of all the faces I have seen, the strong, the silent, the smiling, and I pray that we will find the courage to replace performance with purpose, competition with compassion, and noise with depth.

Because when photos fade, and the lights go out, only the truth of who we are will remain.

And in that truth lies the real wealth of our humanity.

Reflection

But when applause replaces empathy, even grief becomes performance.

Chapter 3: Death, Birthdays, and the Only Time People Speak

The Selective Voices of Community

There is something strange about the way modern communities communicate. People can stay quiet for years, scrolling past one another's posts, ignoring cries for help, yet the moment someone dies, their name floods every group chat. "Rest in peace," "Gone too soon," "We will miss you." Then, as if rehearsed, a long silence follows.

We have become experts at showing up when it no longer matters.

When it's a birthday, people emerge again, typing cheerful messages, sometimes out of habit, sometimes out of guilt. "Happy birthday, long time!" they say, attaching emojis and hearts, though they haven't spoken to the person in years. The gesture looks kind, but under it often hides something hollow.

I have wondered many times what people's intentions are in such moments. Are they genuinely wishing well, or just performing their part in the unwritten social script? Is it love, or is it obligation disguised as kindness?

It feels like a new form of arrogance, the arrogance of selective attention. We offer care only when it is convenient, when the moment feels light or dramatic enough to make us look human. We have learned to time our compassion for effect.

When people pop in only to say "Happy birthday" or "RIP," they unknowingly reveal the state of our relationships. The message is not, "I care about you," but "I see you from afar, and this is the safest distance for me." It is care without commitment. It is empathy without effort.

The New Etiquette of Distance

Across African, Asian, and even Western diaspora communities, this pattern repeats itself. We have replaced consistent relationships with moments of visibility. Instead of walking with people through their storms, we show up at the beginning or the end. We celebrate or mourn, nothing in between.

A South African friend once told me, **"People are no longer emotionally available; they are event available."** That statement stayed with me. Event availability means we show up for visible moments: birthdays, weddings, funerals, graduations. But we disappear for invisible ones: depression, divorce, disappointment, or the daily struggle to keep going.

We have built emotional calendars instead of emotional connections.

The irony is that people genuinely believe they are maintaining friendships by posting on birthdays or writing long eulogies when someone dies. But true connection cannot be preserved through occasional words. It needs presence, patience, and participation.

Many justify their absence by saying life is busy, messages are too much, and they don't know what to say anymore. And yes, life is demanding. Messages pile up. Notifications blur together. But it is not time that kills connection, it is intention. We always find time for what matters.

A Kenyan entrepreneur once told me, "The way people handle friendship now feels like customer service. You only hear from them when they need to maintain the relationship metrics." He was right. Many of us treat relationships as algorithms. We check in just enough to appear decent but never enough to make a difference.

The Overload of Messages

Part of the problem is that we are all drowning in information. Every day, we receive countless updates, opinions, and requests. People share their wins, losses, heartbreaks, and random thoughts. It is a lot to digest. So, to cope, many choose selective engagement. They skim through, react with an emoji, or remain silent.

But silence is not neutral. It shapes people's confidence and mental health. When someone repeatedly shares something personal and receives no response, they eventually stop sharing. They start believing that their pain is inconvenient, their joy irrelevant. And that is how emotional isolation begins.

I once heard from a Ghanaian mother living in Canada who said, "I post only birthdays and obituaries now because people say I talk too much when I post about struggles." Her statement broke my heart. When truth becomes too heavy for others to handle, it pushes honest voices into hiding.

And so, what remains in the group chats and timelines are surface-level exchanges, the polished photos, the predictable greetings, and the occasional condolences. We have learned to celebrate and sympathize but not to support.

The Ethics of Selective Silence

Some people defend their silence as a form of emotional self-care. "I'm choosing my battles," they say. "I can't carry everyone's problems." That is fair. Boundaries are healthy. But boundaries should protect peace, not excuse indifference. There is a difference between resting and withdrawing, between protecting yourself and disconnecting from others' humanity.

I have watched good-hearted people stop speaking truth because their honesty was misinterpreted as bitterness. I have seen those who once stood for justice begin to self-censor because they felt alone. When communities reject truth-tellers, they don't just silence a person; they silence conscience.

A Ugandan friend told me about a WhatsApp group of former classmates. One man shared his frustration about how the group only came alive for funerals. He poured out his heart, calling for real engagement, real help for struggling members. Instead of support, he was told, "Why are you being negative? This group is for fun." He left quietly. Months later, when he passed away, the same group filled with his photos and prayers.

That is the sickness of our times. We wake up when it's too late.

We have mastered the art of emotional timing, saying the right words at the wrong time. We post eulogies for people we ignored while they lived. We comfort families we never checked on. We donate to burials we never supported in life.

We have become a culture of late compassion.

The Currency of Condolences

In many cultures, especially African and Caribbean ones, condolences have become a kind of social currency. When someone dies, the measure of their worth is suddenly determined by how many people show up or post about them. People attend funerals not out of closeness, but out of reputation. "We must be seen there," they say.

It is not unique to Africa. I saw the same pattern in Germany, where colleagues who barely spoke to a man suddenly gathered to praise him after his passing. One woman whispered to me, "It's just what we do." But that phrase, "It's just what we do," is where the problem begins.

Routine empathy is not real empathy. It is performance.

The same applies to birthday greetings. People who haven't exchanged a single meaningful word in years will flood someone's page with glittering wishes. "More blessings!" "Long life!" "God did it again!" And then vanish until next year.

There is nothing wrong with celebration, but celebration without connection is empty. When we wish people well only on their birthdays, what are we really saying? That they matter for twenty-four hours?

A woman from Botswana once told me, "My phone only rings twice a year, my birthday and when someone dies." She laughed as she said it, but her eyes were sad. We live in an era of contact without closeness.

When Truth Becomes Uncomfortable

There are those who still try to speak up. They notice the emptiness, the selective attention, and the hypocrisy. They speak not to shame but to awaken. Yet they often face resistance. Communities do not like mirrors. When someone points out the truth, people label them as angry or ungrateful.

I remember a conversation in a multicultural group chat where one man spoke passionately about how people ignore real suffering. His tone was raw, his words honest. Instead of engaging, others told him to "relax" and "focus on positive vibes." Later, he told me privately, "It's strange that people fight for mental health awareness but cannot handle an honest conversation."

He was right. We have confused positivity with maturity. True emotional intelligence is not avoiding discomfort; it is sitting with it. Communities that cannot handle truth will eventually drown in pretence.

When Emotional Intelligence Goes Missing

Emotional intelligence is the ability to understand not only how others feel, but why they feel that way. It is knowing when to speak, when to listen, and when silence helps instead of hurts. Sadly, this skill is fading. Many now confuse avoidance for wisdom and indifference for strength.

In our attempt to protect our peace, we have built walls too thick for love to pass through. We call it self-care, but sometimes it is just numbness wearing perfume.

There is a growing sickness in communities, the sickness of emotional imbalance. Some people overfeel, others underfeel. Some give endlessly until they collapse; others withhold until they forget how to care. Somewhere in between lies the truth we have lost.

When people who once cared deeply begin to withdraw, it is not always because they stopped believing. Sometimes they are just tired of caring alone. They are tired of watching others wake up only for funerals and birthdays, tired of pretending that routine greetings mean connection.

And slowly, as empathy fades, communities start to rot quietly from within.

The Silent Collapse

The consequences are everywhere. Young people dropping out of school. NEETs, not in education, employment, or training, stuck at home. Families breaking down from invisible financial and emotional strain. Parents hiding depression behind smiles. Adults pretending to have everything together while sinking deeper into loneliness.

And the communities that could help? Too busy watching, too polite to ask, too numb to care.

We are living through an epidemic of polite neglect.

Relearning Presence in a Noisy World

The hardest thing to face about our current world is how emotionally absent we have become while pretending to be present. We are surrounded by people, messages, and notifications, yet true connection is becoming rare. We are busy being visible but not truly available. Communities everywhere are silently falling apart, not because of poverty or politics, but because of neglect disguised as busyness.

When was the last time you looked someone in the eyes and asked, "How are you, really?" When was the last time you listened long enough to hear what they did not say? These are small questions, but they can save lives.

The Arrogance of Routine Kindness

It sounds harsh, but it is true: many acts of kindness today are empty rituals. People pop in to say "Happy birthday" because it makes them feel good, not because they truly remember or care. The message is a digital handshake, not a human touch. The same happens when tragedy strikes. Suddenly, people who have ignored you for years start sharing your photo, writing long paragraphs about how "you were always so kind," when in truth, they never truly knew you.

I once asked a group during a leadership training, "Why do people wait for death to express love?" A man from Kenya replied, "Because death is safe. The person can't reject your message." Everyone fell silent. His answer was uncomfortable but true. It is easier to mourn than to maintain.

We say "RIP" freely because it costs us nothing. Real support, however, demands presence, and presence costs time, emotion, and humility.

This performative kindness creates a subtle arrogance. We believe our short messages are enough to sustain relationships. We think we have done our part, but in reality, we have done the bare minimum.

There is nothing wrong with wishing someone a happy birthday or expressing sympathy. The problem is when these moments replace deeper communication. Relationships cannot thrive on ceremonial attention.

The Fear of Genuine Engagement

Many people avoid deeper engagement because they fear it will make them responsible. When someone shares their pain, listening means acknowledging it. And acknowledging it means you cannot pretend not to know. So we hide behind polite distance.

I remember a man from Tanzania who said, "When I see someone suffering, I scroll past quickly so I don't have to feel guilty." His honesty startled me, but it revealed something crucial. People avoid emotional engagement because it makes them confront their own humanity.

Yet true compassion begins where comfort ends. We cannot claim to be a community while ignoring the emotional and psychological weight people carry.

We must learn to engage again, to be available without being intrusive, to listen without judgment, and to respond without waiting for perfection. Some people do not need us to solve their problems. They just need us to sit beside them while they face them.

Why Truth-Tellers Grow Tired

Every community needs truth-tellers, those who refuse to let silence win. But these people often become the most misunderstood. They speak up when others prefer to stay comfortable. They call for accountability, for empathy, for realness. But in return, they are branded as difficult or dramatic.

I once met a woman from Zimbabwe who said, "I used to speak up about things in my church and community, but people said I was spoiling the mood. Now I just watch." Her eyes were sad but calm, the calm of someone who has learned to retreat for survival.

When truth is rejected long enough, silence becomes the only safe language. That silence, though, is not peace. It is resignation. Communities that silence their truth-tellers eventually lose their moral compass.

We must begin to listen again, even when what is said makes us uncomfortable. A healthy community does not agree on everything, but it listens deeply. Disagreement handled with respect builds trust. Pretending everything is fine destroys it.

When Emotional Intelligence Fails

Emotional intelligence is not about being nice all the time. It is about understanding what people need at the moment and responding with wisdom. Sometimes people need encouragement, other times they need correction, and often they just need to be heard.

Yet today, many use emotional intelligence as an excuse for avoidance. They say, "I'm protecting my peace," but what they mean is, "I don't want to deal with this." Real emotional maturity is not escaping discomfort; it is navigating it with grace.

When communities lose emotional intelligence, conversations become shallow. People misread one another, react too quickly, and take offense too easily. As a result, those who once cared start second-guessing themselves. They begin to wonder, "Should I say anything at all?" Over time, they stop trying.

Once empathy begins to disappear, bitterness starts to grow. People who used to serve with joy begin to feel unappreciated. They start saying, "Why should I bother?" And slowly, a coldness spreads.

This emotional fatigue is dangerous. It makes people numb, and numbness kills community.

How Communities Get Sick

A community becomes sick not overnight, but through a slow erosion of empathy. It starts with silence, then indifference, then competition. Soon, everyone is performing strength while secretly breaking. People begin to measure relationships by convenience.

In cities from Germany to Toronto, from Cameroon to London, I have seen this sickness take root. People gather for celebrations, but not for soul care. They are quick to post, slow to visit. Quick to talk, slow to listen. And all the while, emotional wounds deepen unseen.

The most dangerous sickness in any community is not hatred but apathy. Hatred can be confronted; apathy hides behind smiles.

When we no longer notice the struggles of others, we lose our humanity. When we stop asking, "Who didn't show up and why?" we lose our sensitivity. When we become comfortable with selective empathy, we create a culture of quiet decay.

The Cure: Relearning Presence

Healing begins with presence. Not gifts, not speeches, not posts. Presence. Being there. Sitting with someone without rushing the moment. Asking questions not for gossip but for understanding.

Presence is what builds trust. It is what restores broken confidence. It is what makes people believe again that they are seen.

A young man in Sweden once told me that he was on the verge of suicide when a friend noticed he had stopped replying to messages and decided to visit him. "She didn't come to fix me," he said. "She just sat with me for hours. That visit saved me."

That is the power of presence.

We can relearn this art. It begins by noticing small things. Who has gone quiet in your group? Who always shows up but never speaks? Who stopped posting altogether? These are often signs of struggle. A simple check-in can be a lifeline.

Moving Beyond the Performance of Care

Communities need to stop performing care and start practicing it. That means consistency over ceremony. It means showing up without waiting for birthdays or burials. It means giving before you are asked, listening before you respond, and loving before it becomes convenient.

Real care is quiet. It is not for display. It shows up in groceries delivered, in shared meals, in late-night calls, in unannounced visits that say, "You matter."

When communities practice such care, they heal. Because where people feel seen, they begin to breathe again.

Rebuilding Emotional Intelligence

Emotional intelligence can be relearned. It begins with humility. We must accept that we have all failed someone at some point. We have all missed cues, ignored messages, or stayed silent when we should have spoken. But awareness is the first step toward change.

From there, we can rebuild empathy by being intentional. Ask more questions. Listen without preparing your reply. Offer help without waiting for perfection. Recognize that everyone you meet is fighting a battle you may never see.

We can also create spaces for open dialogue, where people can share without fear of being labeled dramatic or weak. Emotional safety is the soil where authentic community grows.

The Power of a Small Circle

Sometimes healing begins with a small circle of genuine people. Not everyone will understand your heart, and that is fine. What matters is finding those who do. Two or three sincere friends who check in, who pray with you, who tell you the truth even when it stings, are worth more than a thousand online followers.

In an age of superficiality, small circles create depth. They allow honesty to breathe again. They teach us that intimacy is not about quantity but quality.

When We Remember Again

Imagine if every community, every group chat, every family decided to remember each other beyond ceremonies. Imagine if the same energy used for condolences and birthday wishes was used to check on mental health, education, and purpose.

Imagine if we stopped waiting for the D-word, death, before expressing love. Imagine if our messages of care arrived while people could still read them.

That vision is not unrealistic. It begins with one decision at a time: to notice, to ask, to listen, to show up.

When people begin to care again with sincerity, communities start to heal. Birthdays become genuine celebrations, not performances. Funerals become reflections, not regrets. Truth becomes welcome again.

And slowly, we move from a world of selective voices to one of steady presence.

Because real love does not wait for an occasion. It lives every day in the quiet choices we make to see, to care, and to stay.

When Help Hurts

In one of my alumni groups, after years of leading, organizing, and caring for everyone, I faced a moment that broke something inside me. One of my closest friends passed away, and her death silenced me in ways I could not explain. It was as if I had been speaking into an empty room for years, giving my time and energy, hoping to make people see each other again. But when she died, I realized there truly is a time for everything.

Grief has a way of peeling off illusions. It reveals who listens, who pretends, who genuinely cares, and who simply waits for the next event. Even in the middle of mourning, I found myself misunderstood. When I tried to express my pain, my truth, and the lessons I had learned through loss, some of my mates labeled me as dramatic. Others tried to hush me. It was as if honesty itself had become offensive.

One would think grief earns empathy, but often it earns discomfort. People are uneasy with emotion they cannot control. They rush to fix what they do not understand. I remember one friend in particular, a good woman with the best of intentions. She wanted to help me, but her help came heavy. She spoke over me instead of listening. She offered solutions when I needed silence. She imposed her version of healing, insisting it was for my good.

That experience taught me a hard truth: not everyone knows how to help.

Some help from a place of genuine compassion. Others help from their own unresolved pain. When people have not healed, they project their brokenness into their kindness. It becomes a kind of tension help, a rescue that doesn't offer peace or joy. You can feel their anxiety pressing against your sadness, their need to be the savior overshadowing your need to be seen.

It is a confusing form of comfort. You are grateful yet exhausted. They say, "I'm just helping," but their help feels like a storm you must survive.

The Weight of Misguided Help

In that alumni group, I began to see how often communities confuse helping with controlling. Some people want to fix others so they don't have to face their own discomfort. They offer advice not because they understand, but because silence scares them. They mean well, but their help becomes invasive, loud, and hurried.

Real help listens before acting. It asks, "What do you need?" instead of assuming it knows. It does not compete with pain or rush it into recovery. It allows healing to move at its own pace.

I realized my friend's efforts were more about her than about me. She could not stand seeing someone in pain without trying to repair it instantly. But sometimes, the kindest thing a person can do is sit beside you and admit, "I don't know how to fix this, but I'm here."

We live in a culture that glorifies action and solutions, so sitting still with someone's sorrow feels strange. Yet that is often where true help begins.

The Silence After Speaking

When I finally gathered the courage to share what I felt in the group, I expected understanding. Instead, I was met with polite silence. Some avoided me altogether, afraid my words would remind them of their own losses. Others said I was "too emotional." A few tried to smooth things over by changing the topic. It was a quiet rejection, but a deep one.

For days, I questioned myself. Was I wrong to speak? Was I too honest? Did my vulnerability make people uncomfortable?

Then I remembered: truth always disturbs the surface before it brings healing. Those who cannot face their own feelings will often silence the ones who try. My mistake was assuming that everyone in the group wanted depth. Many only wanted distraction.

Still, the experience helped me understand community in a new way. It showed me that people interpret care differently. Some equate silence with respect, others with neglect. Some think leadership means always being strong, never showing cracks. But the truth is, strength without softness becomes cruelty.

The Lessons Hidden in Pain

That season of misunderstanding taught me more about love than years of easy friendship ever could. I learned that maturity is not just knowing when to speak, but also when to stop explaining yourself. It is accepting that not everyone will understand your journey, and that's all right.

It also taught me that help without listening is harm wrapped in affection. Not every kind act heals. Some actions, though dressed as help, only deepen wounds because they lack empathy.

Helping someone requires humility, the courage to set aside your ego and meet them where they are. It is saying, "I don't need to be the hero here; I just want you to know you're not alone." That is the kind of help that restores, not overwhelms.

Choosing Stillness

After that experience, I chose stillness. I stepped back from constant leadership and learned to breathe again. I stopped forcing people to understand and began to value the few who already did.

Sometimes, stepping back is not quitting; it is protecting your peace from those who confuse your passion for drama. I learned that silence can be healing when it comes from choice, not suppression.

In my quiet moments, I thought about that friend who imposed her way of helping. I realized she, too, was doing her best with the tools she had. Her methods came from her own unhealed places. And in that recognition, I found forgiveness. Because even misguided help is still a sign that someone tried.

Redefining Help

If there is one thing this journey has taught me, it is that real help is not about doing more but about being more present. It is not about fixing others but standing beside them. It is not about giving what makes you feel good, but offering what brings peace to the one in pain.

Communities can only heal when people learn the difference between helping and healing. Helping is action; healing is presence. The first can be noisy; the second is often silent.

When we begin to understand this, our relationships transform. We stop trying to prove our usefulness and start practicing gentleness. We stop measuring love by effort and start measuring it by understanding.

Finding Meaning Again

As I think back to that group, to the laughter, the tension, and the unspoken lessons, I no longer feel bitter. I feel aware. I know now that every community mirrors the people within it, imperfect, learning, sometimes blind, but still capable of grace.

Perhaps the goal is not to build perfect communities but honest ones. Ones where people can say, "I'm not okay," and not fear judgment. Where leaders can grieve without losing respect. Where help does not wound, and silence does not mean indifference.

Because in the end, life will always bring both birthdays and burials, laughter and loss. What matters is not when people show up, but how they show up.

And I have learned that the greatest gift we can offer one another is not applause or advice. It is presence, patience, and the quiet humility to help without hurting.

Reflection

Eventually, some stop performing altogether. They disappear, not because they want to, but because nobody notices when they fade.

Everyone Might be Smiling, But Nobody's Okay

Chapter 4: The Disappearing Ones

People Who Stop Talking but No One Checks In

There is a quiet kind of disappearance that happens every day, and most of us do not even notice it. Someone who used to speak often stops posting. Someone who attended every meeting suddenly misses two, then three, then all. Their name slips from the conversation, and the group moves on. We tell ourselves they are busy, that they need space, that they are probably fine. But sometimes, that silence is not healing. It is a cry that went unheard.

We live in an age that mistakes absence for strength. When someone withdraws, we assume they are resting, reflecting, or sorting things out. It is a comforting explanation, but not always true. Sometimes silence is not peace but exhaustion. Sometimes people disappear not because they are recharging, but because they are running out of reasons to stay visible.

I have seen this too many times. People vanish from community groups, church gatherings, or alumni circles, and no one checks in. There is a general understanding that everyone is fighting their own battles, and that respecting privacy means staying quiet. But respect without compassion is neglect. Checking on people who disappear should not be an intrusion; it should be part of our communal rhythm.

Quiet Exits from Chats, Meetings, Even Life

Across Europe, there have been countless stories of Africans in the diaspora found dead in their apartments, sometimes weeks later. The discovery often starts with a smell, a neighbor's complaint, or an unanswered knock. And when the authorities finally open the door, they find a life that ended quietly, without witness or farewell.

These were not strangers to us. They were our brothers, sisters, uncles, and friends. People with family members back home waiting for remittances, for the next phone call, for the next holiday visit. Families who proudly said, "He's doing well abroad," never realizing their loved one had already gone.

I remember reading a story from France about a Ghanaian man named Kojo who had been living alone for ten years. He worked as a cleaner, sent money home faithfully, and never missed a month. When he suddenly stopped calling, his family assumed his schedule had changed. They waited. They left voice messages. It took three months before someone in the local Ghanaian association decided to visit. They found him lying in his bed, gone for weeks.

That story haunted me. It reminded me that death often comes quietly, while we are busy assuming others are fine.

And it is not just Africans abroad. In Japan, there is a word, *kodokushi*, which means "lonely death." Thousands of elderly people die alone each year, their bodies discovered only after the smell alerts neighbors.

In London, one of the most haunting cases was that of **Joyce Carol Vincent**, a British woman who died in her apartment in

2003 and was not discovered until **January 25, 2006**. She was just 38 years old. Joyce had been a vibrant woman, described as elegant and friendly, with a circle of acquaintances from different walks of life. When her body was found, her television was still on, tuned to BBC One. Her mail had piled up behind the door, and parts of her bills were still being paid automatically from her bank account.

The neighbors assumed the flat was empty. The building was noisy, and the smell that occasionally drifted through the hallway was blamed on nearby bins. No one questioned the continuous sound of her television because, in a city like London, constant noise is ordinary.

When the authorities entered her apartment, they found her remains surrounded by Christmas presents she had been wrapping. She had died quietly, possibly of an asthma attack, alone, unseen. For nearly three years, her life continued administratively but not physically.

Her story became a painful symbol of modern isolation, how one can live in one of the world's busiest cities and still vanish without notice.

And this is not an isolated story. Across every continent, people are fading into silence while surrounded by millions.

How Depression Hides in Plain Sight

Depression rarely announces itself. It disguises itself as busyness, as withdrawal, as "I'm just tired." It hides behind smiles and polite replies. People keep up appearances until the energy runs out. By the time they disappear, it is often too late.

In a Kenyan community in the Netherlands, there was a young man named Brian who was always the life of the party. He cracked jokes, organized barbecues, played soccer on weekends. One day he simply stopped coming. His friends thought he had gotten a new job. Weeks later, they learned he had taken his own life. At the memorial, everyone kept asking the same question: "How did we miss the signs?"

The signs were there. They always are. But signs require attention, and attention requires intention.

In Lagos, I met a woman who said something profound: "Depression is not just sadness; it's disappearing slowly while people keep clapping." She was right. Many people are celebrated publicly and crumbling privately.

Sometimes the person who disappears is not physically gone but emotionally absent. They attend meetings but say nothing. They laugh without joy. They perform, then retreat. Yet nobody asks, "Are you okay?"

Real Stories of Those Who Felt Invisible Until It Was Too Late

A woman in Canada told me about her friend from Uganda who used to post Bible verses every morning. Then one week, the posts stopped. At first, no one noticed. Then, after a few months, someone finally sent a message. Her husband replied, saying she had passed from cancer weeks earlier. He added, "She didn't want to bother anyone." Those words cut deep. She didn't want to bother anyone.

That is how quiet many people's pain has become, polite, disciplined, almost apologetic. They don't want to inconvenience others with their suffering.

We all have our own battles, yes, but the truth is that kindness is not a resource we run out of. Checking on people is not charity. It is humanity. It is the quiet work of empathy.

How Communities Can Intentionally Notice

Communities must make noticing part of their structure. A simple message that says, "You crossed my mind today," can break through the loneliness that depression builds. A short voice note can remind someone they exist beyond their struggles.

A man in Malaysia told me that he was on the edge of despair after losing his job during the pandemic. He had not eaten for two days when his old university friend suddenly called just to ask how he was doing. That call, he said, "felt like air returning to my lungs." He didn't need money that day; he needed acknowledgment. He needed to be seen.

In South Africa, a young woman said she had been contemplating ending her life when her church leader texted her out of nowhere: "I just wanted you to know you are valuable." That small message changed her mind. She said later, "I felt like God had remembered me through that message."

We underestimate how powerful small acts of attention are. A call that doesn't ask for anything, a visit without an agenda, a text sent out of genuine thought, these things regulate hearts that are racing with anxiety. They stabilize minds running toward dark thoughts. They calm nervous systems at their breaking point.

The Rhythm of Empathy

There is something sacred about noticing absence. In the old African village, when someone didn't come to fetch water, others asked. When a child was missing from play, elders asked. When a fire didn't light in a family's hut, neighbors checked. Presence was communal; so was concern.

But in today's world, we mistake digital awareness for connection. We see people online and assume they are alive and well. We count their likes and think we know their lives. We forget that online visibility is not proof of inner vitality.

When someone stops showing up, it should raise our curiosity, not our suspicion. It should move us to check in, not gossip.

There is a Swahili saying, *"Mtu ni watu"* meaning a person is people. It means no one truly exists alone. Our survival depends on one another. The disappearing ones are not weak; they are human. They remind us that strength is not endless, that everyone reaches a breaking point.

We must create cultures where disappearance triggers care, not curiosity. Where absence becomes everyone's concern, not just gossip material.

Because sometimes, the only thing standing between a person and despair is one call that says, "You are not forgotten."

Reflection

Yet sometimes, the same silence that isolates can also whisper an invitation to mentor, to guide, to check in.

Everyone Might be Smiling, But Nobody's Okay

Chapter 5: When Mentorship Becomes Lifesaving

The Power of a Call, a Job Lead, a Small Opening

Sometimes help does not arrive as money or rescue. It comes as a voice, a message, a simple act of noticing. One thoughtful call at the right moment can change the course of a person's life. It can stop a decision, restore courage, or remind someone that they still matter.

But there is also wisdom in how we reach out. This is not an invitation to start calling everyone in the name of care. It is a reminder to live with awareness. We all have circles, small or large, where we already belong. The real test of compassion begins within those familiar spaces. It is about consistency, not quantity.

Checking in on people is sacred work, but it must be done ethically and thoughtfully. It is not curiosity dressed as care or pity disguised as purpose. It is the genuine act of reaching out because something within you says, "This person needs light today."

There are times when the thought of someone crosses your mind suddenly, almost spiritually. Moments later, you might hear news about them, good or bad. Those thoughts are not always random. They are often gentle nudges of responsibility. When someone's name flashes through your heart, it may be time to reach out. A single message saying, "You came to mind today, I hope you're well," can complete a circle of grace you did not even know was open.

The Quiet Power of Discernment

True empathy is not impulsive; it is discerning. You do not have to call everyone. You only need to listen when compassion whispers. There is a rhythm to human connection that cannot be forced. Some calls will be meant for encouragement, others for listening, and sometimes, for simple presence.

A South African entrepreneur once told me how a single call changed his destiny. "I was on the verge of closing my business," he said. "My mentor called that day just to ask how I was holding up. I told him everything was fine, but he could hear the fatigue in my voice. He didn't give me money. He gave me perspective." That conversation became the pivot that helped him restructure his company. Two years later, he was employing others.

Mentorship, in its purest form, is not just about teaching skills or giving advice. It is the art of staying connected to another person's journey in a way that honors their growth. It is relational, not transactional.

Mentorship as a Two-Way Street

Many people think mentorship only benefits the one being guided, but true mentorship transforms both sides. It keeps the mentor grounded, aware of new realities, and constantly learning empathy. For the mentee, it brings direction, confidence, and belonging.

I once met a young woman from Rwanda named Liliane who worked as a cleaner in Germany. She dreamed of starting her own catering business but had no idea where to begin. Her mentor, an older Ghanaian woman, began meeting with her once a month for tea. They talked about budgeting, pricing, and networking. The mentor introduced her to two clients who helped launch her career. Five years later, Liliane was employing three people.

When I asked her mentor why she helped, she said, "Because someone once did the same for me when I could not see my own potential." That is the essence of mentorship, paying forward the grace that once found you.

Mentorship is not always formal. Sometimes it is hidden in friendship, in consistent check-ins, in sharing opportunities. The moment two people decide to walk together toward growth, mentorship has begun.

When Mentorship Saves a Life

There are stories of mentorship that go beyond success; they touch survival. A Nigerian man in Finland once shared that his mentor's consistent messages during a dark season kept him from giving up. "Every Sunday, he would text me: 'Remember your purpose.' I never replied for months, but I never deleted them. When I finally got better, I called him. He said he had felt a strong urge to keep writing, even when I didn't respond. That saved me."

In India, a mentor-mentee relationship between two women began when one offered a job referral during lockdown. What started as a professional link became a lifeline. The mentee later confessed she had been silently struggling with depression and that the new job, and the trust it carried, gave her a reason to keep going.

These are not dramatic rescues. They are quiet, ordinary miracles, one person's intentional effort rewriting another person's life story.

Boundaries and Respect in Reaching Out

Compassion must always be paired with respect. Not everyone wants deep engagement. Some people are private, and others are not ready to share. Checking in does not mean demanding disclosure. It means offering space.

There is a way to care that honors dignity. You do not have to ask invasive questions. Sometimes all it takes is saying, "I'm thinking of you. No need to reply if you're tired." That sentence alone can comfort someone who feels pressured to explain their silence.

The line between care and control can be thin. The best mentors and friends understand that people grow best when they feel safe, not scrutinized. Emotional boundaries protect the sanctity of connection.

A Kenyan pastor once said, "Compassion without discretion can cause damage." He was right. Not every call needs to turn into counseling. Not every text needs a response. The goal is presence, not performance.

The Spiritual Timing of Care

There are moments in life when care arrives with divine timing. You think of someone for no reason, then later learn they were in distress at that exact moment. These patterns remind us that human relationships often move in rhythms unseen.

I once experienced it myself. A man I had mentored years earlier suddenly came to mind one morning. I felt the urge to send him a brief message: "Stay strong, something good is coming." Hours later, he replied, "How did you know? I just lost my job this morning." The timing stunned me. It reminded me that compassion is often guided by forces we do not fully understand.

It is not about being spiritual for the sake of appearance. It is about staying sensitive to the quiet prompts of conscience and faith. When we act on those small nudges, we participate in a larger story of grace.

Why One Person's Effort Can Rewrite a Life Story

We underestimate the ripple effect of one person's intention. A mentor who offers a job referral can alter the direction of a family's future. A businessperson who takes a chance on a young intern can ignite an entire career. A simple introduction can open a world of possibilities.

Every act of guidance carries invisible consequences. We do not always see the full fruit of our mentorship, but that does not make it less powerful. The person you help today might one day help someone you will never meet. That is how legacies are built, quietly, one act of kindness at a time.

Mentorship as Community Healing

When mentorship becomes a habit within communities, transformation follows. It breaks the culture of competition and replaces it with connection. It turns gossip into guidance and envy into empowerment. It creates a rhythm where everyone has someone to look up to and someone to lift.

A healthy community is one where no one feels entirely alone. When we mentor and check on each other ethically, we build networks of emotional and professional safety. It is not about being saviors. It is about being available.

The African proverb says, *"If you want to go fast, go alone. If you want to go far, go together."* That wisdom applies not just to travel but to survival. We go further when we remember one another.

The Gentle Call to Awareness

As you read this, perhaps someone's name comes to mind. Maybe a friend you haven't spoken to in a while, or a young person who once asked for your guidance. You don't need to make a grand gesture. Just start small. Send a message. Ask a question. Offer a word of encouragement.

Mentorship does not always happen in meetings or programs. It happens in moments, a text, a call, a conversation that carries warmth instead of judgment. Those moments are the lifelines that tie us back to our humanity.

Checking in ethically means respecting timing, boundaries, and truth. It means listening for the quiet cues of conscience that say, "Now." It is not about how many people you call. It is about how sincerely you care.

Because sometimes, one small, well-timed connection can be the difference between despair and hope, between giving up and beginning again.

And in that simple act, one human being becomes the echo of divine compassion for another.

Reflection

Still, many communities mistake movement for meaning, gathering without growing.

Chapter 6: Unmasking the Culture of Performance

The Pressure to Pretend

The power of mentorship and genuine care always exposes what performance tries to hide. After every wave of connection, you start to see clearly the difference between people who gather to grow and those who gather to impress. Somewhere between alumni groups, church circles, and social clubs, community lost its heartbeat and became a stage.

Performance has become the default posture of modern society. Everyone is performing something: success, stability, happiness, faith, or generosity. We show up to events dressed in competence, not comfort. We talk about impact but measure applause. We celebrate the image of togetherness while quietly avoiding the work of truth.

In many alumni groups, the measure of belonging has shifted from sincerity to spectacle. Those who attend every event and post the most photos are seen as the most loyal. Those who question direction or purpose are branded as difficult. The pressure to pretend is constant. It is exhausting, but we keep doing it because the cost of honesty seems too high.

I remember attending a reunion lately where everything looked perfect. The décor sparkled, the laughter was loud, and everyone called each other "family." Yet the moment someone mentioned accountability, the air shifted. Smiles tightened.

Conversations changed. Because accountability demands depth, and depth exposes what performance hides.

We have become experts in attendance but amateurs in authenticity. We know how to show up, but not how to show care.

How People Measure Value by Image, Not Impact

Image has become the new currency of credibility. The person who looks successful is often believed to be more capable than the one quietly working behind the scenes. We have built a generation of visual achievers, people whose validation depends on visibility.

In church circles, the same pattern appears. The members who sing loudest, dress best, or give publicly often gain respect faster than the ones who serve quietly in the background. In social clubs, leadership positions sometimes go to those who project wealth, not wisdom. Even in alumni groups, influence often belongs to the loudest contributor, not the most thoughtful one.

I once met a man from Kenya who told me he stopped attending his alumni meetings because they had become more like fashion shows than fellowships. "Every gathering felt like a competition," he said. "If you didn't arrive in a luxury car or bring a donation, no one really spoke to you." His words were sad but familiar. The culture of optics had swallowed the culture of purpose.

This obsession with image is not new, but social media has made it louder. We now compare our behind-the-scenes struggles with other people's highlight reels. The danger is that when communities start performing success, they stop pursuing substance. Appearances become achievements, and presence becomes enough to earn applause.

But the truth is, visibility without value is emptiness in disguise. The people who truly shape communities are often the quiet builders, the ones who don't post every move but keep showing up with consistency. They may not have the spotlight, but they carry the structure.

The Need to Shift from Attendance to Accountability

Attendance fills seats; accountability fills hearts. The difference between a gathering that grows and one that fades is accountability. Without it, meetings become rituals and events become performances.

I have seen it in countless spaces: alumni networks that meet monthly but never grow, church committees that plan endlessly but never act, clubs that celebrate anniversaries but ignore impact. The structure looks alive, but the soul is gone. Everyone is busy doing, yet nothing changes.

Accountability asks the uncomfortable questions: Why are we meeting? Who benefits? What has improved because we gathered? It is the discipline of purpose. It reminds us that unity without direction is just noise.

One of the most powerful moments I ever witnessed was in a small professional group in Toronto. Instead of the usual agenda, the moderator asked everyone to share one real struggle and one real win from their month. At first, there was awkward silence. But then, one woman spoke up about losing her job. Another admitted he was battling burnout. The tone of the meeting changed completely. The group became human again.

By the end, members were exchanging job leads and prayer requests. It was no longer about showing up; it was about showing up honestly. That is what accountability looks like, a space where truth is safe and pretense is unnecessary.

Signs Your Group Is All Show and No Soul

If your community looks busy but feels hollow, you might be trapped in the culture of performance. The signs are subtle at first, but they always reveal themselves over time.

1. The focus is on events, not impact.
If every meeting ends with photos but no measurable progress, your group is performing, not growing. Impact is what happens after the event, not during it.

2. Vulnerability is avoided.
When people who express pain or frustration are labeled as negative or dramatic, it means the culture values comfort over truth. Real communities allow people to be real.

3. Giving replaces growing.
In some groups, the biggest donors dominate every conversation, while the ones who need support sit quietly in the back. True giving builds others, not egos.

4. Leadership becomes a title, not a responsibility.
When leaders love control more than care, when they speak often but listen rarely, when their presence is more performative than transformative, the group's foundation is already cracking.

5. Feedback feels like an attack.

Healthy communities embrace feedback as fuel for growth. Unhealthy ones treat it as betrayal. The moment correction becomes conflict, pride has replaced purpose.

6. Attendance matters more than authenticity.

When being seen is valued more than being sincere, when missing a meeting is treated as disloyalty but missing integrity is ignored, then the soul of the group is gone.

These are not just red flags; they are warning signs of slow decay. Groups built on performance eventually collapse under the weight of their own emptiness.

The Courage to Unmask

The most courageous thing any community can do is tell itself the truth. It takes bravery to admit, "We've been performing more than building." It takes maturity to ask, "What are we really doing here?"

Every great revival, spiritual, social, or cultural, begins with honesty. The moment a group chooses substance over spectacle, healing begins.

I once attended a church that decided to cancel its annual conference one year. Instead, they spent the same money to pay off school fees for children of single parents in the congregation. That one act spoke louder than a thousand sermons. It reminded everyone that faith is not about gathering crowds, but about transforming lives.

The same principle applies everywhere. Alumni groups that shift from competition to collaboration become families. Business networks that shift from status to service become movements. Friendships that shift from performance to presence become sanctuaries.

Unmasking the culture of performance is not about exposing others. It is about examining ourselves. It is asking, "Am I here to impress or to impact?" Because the answer to that question determines the health of every relationship, every team, every community.

Returning to the Heart

Real communities breathe. They grow through honesty and heal through compassion. They thrive when members show up not as perfect versions of themselves but as real people with real needs.

When we begin to measure value by impact instead of image, everything changes. Events start having meaning. Relationships gain depth. Accountability replaces appearances.

The greatest shift we can make is from performance to purpose. It is the shift that turns gatherings into growth centers and turns participants into partners.

The world does not need more perfectly curated communities. It needs brave ones, groups unafraid to love truth more than optics, to choose meaning over marketing, and to show up not just with smiles but with substance.

Because when a community finally drops its mask, it doesn't become smaller. It becomes stronger.

Reflection

A group without structure eventually confuses noise for purpose and motion for progress.

Chapter 7: The Crisis of No Structure

When Gatherings Lose Their Way

Every performance eventually fades when there is no structure to hold it up. The applause stops, the music quiets, and what remains is the truth. A group that lives for show without direction eventually collapses under its own weight. This is how many good communities die: not through conflict, but through confusion.

I have seen it too many times. Alumni networks, church committees, family associations, and social clubs begin with enthusiasm. There is energy, laughter, and goodwill. But after a while, meetings become repetitive, goals blur, and conversations circle back to the same points. Everyone keeps showing up, yet nothing moves forward. It feels active, but it is only motion without progress.

The root cause is simple: no structure. When there is no clear vision, a group becomes an echo chamber of good intentions. It may survive for a while on nostalgia or charisma, but without direction, entropy sets in.

Structure is not about control. It is about clarity. It answers the question, "Why are we here?" Without that, even the best intentions scatter like windblown seeds.

Why Groups That "Just Meet" Eventually Die Off

Meetings without purpose are emotional traps. People attend out of loyalty or habit, but deep down, they know nothing meaningful will change. Over time, they stop contributing. Then they stop attending. Eventually, the group fades into silence, remembered only through old photos and halfhearted memories of "how it used to be."

In the beginning, everyone thinks the absence of structure is freedom. "Let's not overcomplicate things," someone says. "We're just here to connect." It sounds noble, even refreshing. But connection without intention soon loses power.

A social club I once joined began with weekly meetups that felt like family. We cooked together, talked about home, and celebrated birthdays. But a year later, attendance began to drop. The conversation grew repetitive, the excitement dimmed. There was no shared project, no common mission. We were together but going nowhere.

Eventually, the group disbanded, not because people stopped caring, but because there was nothing left to care about collectively.

This is how communities die quietly. Not through arguments, but through the slow leak of purpose.

The Danger of Unclear Vision

A vision is what gives a group identity. It is the compass that keeps enthusiasm from wandering. Without it, every idea becomes a distraction and every opinion becomes a battle.

When there is no shared goal, even the smallest differences can cause fractures. One person wants to focus on social activities, another on charity, another on business. Instead of alignment, there is confusion. Everyone means well, but good intentions without direction pull people apart.

I met a young woman who belonged to a women's empowerment group that began with promise. They had skilled members: teachers, nurses, business owners. But there was no unified vision. Each meeting became a debate about what to do next. Should they open a small savings cooperative or start a mentorship program? Months passed with no decision. Eventually, frustration replaced fellowship. Members drifted away one by one until only two remained.

"Everyone wanted to help," she said, "but no one knew what we were helping toward."

Vision is not optional; it is oxygen. Without it, even love and passion run out of breath.

The Cost of Neglecting Talent, Needs, and Calling

Every group holds hidden treasure in its members: unique talents, experiences, and callings. But when a community lacks structure, those treasures remain buried. People show up with potential but have no platform to use it. Over time, they shrink into spectators.

Neglecting the gifts within a group is one of the fastest ways to lose its spirit. People need to feel that they matter, that their contribution makes a difference. When they don't, they begin to withdraw quietly.

In a church committee I once observed, the same three people handled everything: events, finances, announcements. They were hardworking and sincere, but their control left no room for others to grow. Slowly, other members stopped volunteering. Some even left. The group didn't fall apart overnight, but over time, enthusiasm turned to apathy.

The truth is, structure distributes responsibility. It invites participation. It says, "We need you here." Without that invitation, communities become one-man shows or spectator sports.

And it's not just about using talents. It's about understanding needs. Every group has members in transition — people changing jobs, caring for sick parents, dealing with loss, or struggling financially. Without a structured way to identify and support these people, they slip through the cracks.

Structure gives care a system. It ensures that compassion is not just emotional but organized.

When Growth Is Not Intentional

Entropy is the natural state of everything left unattended. Just as a garden becomes overgrown without tending, communities decay without purpose. If you are not growing intentionally, you are shrinking silently.

Growth does not happen by accident. It requires structure, goals, and follow-through. It asks, "What are we building?" and then commits to building it. Without, even the most passionate groups lose momentum.

In London, I met an alumni association that had lasted for over 20 years. When I asked the secret to their longevity, the president smiled and said, "We keep a three-year vision at all times." Every three years, they reviewed their goals, refreshed leadership, and assigned measurable targets: scholarships, mentorship programs, business collaborations. That rhythm of intentional growth kept them alive.

Compare that to another group I encountered in Berlin that was formed around the same time. They had no goals beyond annual parties. At first, it was fun. But eventually, people started asking, "What next?" There was no answer. Within five years, the group dissolved.

Structure is not a cage; it is a spine. It holds the body of a community upright. Without it, even the strongest friendships begin to slump under the weight of disorganization.

Rediscovering Order and Purpose

When a group realizes it has lost structure, that awareness is not defeat; it is an invitation. It means there is still life to rebuild. Structure does not have to be complicated. It can start with three simple questions:

1. Why do we exist?

2. Who are we serving?

3. How do we measure growth?

When these questions are answered honestly, clarity begins to return.

Every group, no matter how lost, can rediscover purpose. A community can decide at any point to start again, to shift from routine to relevance. It begins with leadership willing to listen and members willing to engage.

Structure brings accountability, and accountability revives trust. Trust then fuels creativity, and creativity sustains growth. That is the natural order of a healthy group.

The Hope Beyond Chaos

The death of structure does not have to mean the death of community. It is a warning, not a final sentence. With the right vision, even broken groups can be reborn.

When people realign around purpose, meetings regain meaning. When everyone's gifts find expression, energy returns. When accountability replaces performance, connection deepens.

A community that builds structure around shared purpose becomes unstoppable. It can weather disagreements, endure setbacks, and adapt to change. Because structure turns emotion into movement and dreams into development.

The truth is, most communities don't fail because people stop caring. They fail because caring alone is not enough. Love must be organized.

Without structure, even sincerity loses strength. But with structure, even small beginnings can grow into something extraordinary.

And that is where hope begins again.

Reflection

But every collapse carries a seed of rebuilding, if only we choose to plant it.

Everyone Might be Smiling, But Nobody's Okay

Chapter 8: Rebuilding Community with Substance

When the Show Ends and the Work Begins

After every season of chaos, disillusionment, and quiet collapse, there comes a sacred pause, the moment when we finally admit that performance is not enough. It is in that silence that substance begins to grow.

Communities, like people, can be reborn. But rebirth never happens through more noise or more meetings. It begins with intention. A group that wants to move from survival to significance must learn to build on purpose, not pressure. It must decide to trade applause for accountability and excitement for endurance.

Substance is not glamorous, but it is lasting. It does not always photograph well, but it builds legacies. The communities that stand the test of time are those rooted in clarity, compassion, and consistent action. They are not built on who shouts the loudest, but on who serves the deepest.

True rebuilding begins when a group chooses to ask itself five honest questions, the five elements that form the pillars of substance.

1. Shared Purpose: Why Are We Here?

Without a shared purpose, even the most talented groups drift. Purpose is the north star that directs energy, resources, and relationships toward meaning.

A group can meet for ten years and still not have a shared purpose if everyone defines it differently. One person might think the goal is social connection, another might think it's business networking, another might see it as community service. Without a unified answer, the group becomes a ship sailing in five directions at once.

In one of my alumni groups, I once assumed everyone was seeking growth. I posted thoughtful reflections, project updates, and opportunities for collaboration. Then one day, a very close member told me, "Focus on your projects. Posting too much won't make people read." I paused. It wasn't anger that hit me; it was curiosity. What was the psychology behind that comment?

It made me realize something profound: even among adults who claim to want progress, there are unspoken hierarchies of visibility. Some want to lead, but only from the spotlight. When another person begins to share actively, it threatens the balance of recognition. So instead of encouraging participation, they prefer silence. And yet, when that person finally withdraws, they feel comfortable again, in charge once more.

But purpose cannot thrive in the soil of insecurity. If growth intimidates people, the group will stagnate. Purpose requires space for every voice to be valued, not silenced.

Shared purpose is what transforms meetings into missions. It begins with one honest question: "What are we really trying to build together?" Once that question is answered clearly, every other decision becomes easier.

2. Support System: How Do We Help?

A healthy community must be a safety net, not a stage. It should be the first place people turn to in crisis, not the last. Support must be structured, intentional, and shame-free.

The simplest way to build that structure is to create a transition fund, a small emergency pool that helps members in times of sudden hardship. It doesn't have to be massive; it just needs to be reliable. One unexpected hospital bill, one eviction notice, one job loss can destabilize a person's life. But with a transition fund, no one has to suffer silently.

Support must also go beyond money. It includes mentorship, emotional check-ins, shared resources, and empathy. A community that only knows how to celebrate but not how to comfort will eventually lose its heart.

In Maryland, a small professional circle created a "One Call Away" system. Every member was assigned two people to check on weekly. They didn't need to have long conversations; sometimes, just a "thinking of you" message was enough. Over time, that simple act built trust that outlasted events.

Support is not charity. It is shared responsibility. It is saying, "We will not let you fall unnoticed."

3. Growth Culture: How Do We Get Better?

Growth does not happen by accident; it must be cultivated. Communities that stop learning eventually stop living.

A growth culture is one that values progress over perfection. It encourages members to keep developing spiritually, intellectually, financially, and emotionally. It celebrates effort, not only outcomes.

The challenge is that in many social groups, especially alumni circles, 90 percent of people are silent observers. This is known as the 90-9-1 rule: 90 percent watch, 9 percent engage occasionally, and only 1 percent do the consistent work. That pattern extends to nearly every online and physical community.

But substance demands we shift that ratio. The silent 90 percent are not lazy; many are just waiting to be acknowledged for who they are, not for what others want them to be. They want to contribute, but they need space and encouragement.

Growth culture is not about forcing everyone to act the same. It's about unlocking what's already there. A strong group should make room for diverse expressions of value, the thinker, the doer, the encourager, the silent supporter. Everyone adds something.

When growth becomes collective, progress becomes natural. Instead of competing, people start collaborating. Instead of watching, they start building.

4. Opportunity Pathways: Who Can We Lift?

The mark of a mature community is not how well its leaders succeed but how many others they lift. A community must create pathways for opportunity, mentorship programs, business collaborations, referrals, and skill exchanges.

One of the easiest ways to start is by building a directory. Gather names of mentors, business owners, professionals, and job leads within the group. When someone is in transition, they should not have to start from scratch; they should be able to reach into their community for direction.

Another tool that works is forming accountability pods, small groups of three to five people who check in weekly on goals, projects, or wellbeing. These pods create bonds that large gatherings cannot. They help people grow through consistency and mutual encouragement.

In London, I saw a group that turned these pods into "Success Circles." Each member had to share one weekly win and one weekly challenge. Over time, members began to thrive because they were seen, heard, and supported consistently.

Opportunity pathways are not about handouts; they are about hand-ups. They build a culture where no one has to climb alone.

5. Spiritual Anchor: What Values Hold Us Together?

Every healthy community must have a moral spine. Structure without values is manipulation; progress without principles is emptiness.

A spiritual anchor does not mean preaching or forcing religion into group life. It means agreeing on the values that guide decisions, integrity, compassion, fairness, humility, respect. These are the silent codes that make relationships sustainable.

Without shared values, groups lose direction when conflict arises. People start defending egos instead of the truth. But when there is a spiritual core, disagreements become opportunities for growth, not grounds for division.

I have watched many groups crumble because no one dared to ask, "What kind of people are we becoming?" That question is as vital as "What are we achieving?"

Faith, when applied humbly, brings balance. It reminds us that leadership is service, that compassion is strength, and that no achievement is worth more than human dignity.

How to Start Small

Rebuilding does not need to begin with grandeur. It begins with commitment. A few practical steps can turn good intentions into real transformation:

1. Create a transition fund for emergencies.

2. Build a directory of mentors, business owners, and job leads.

3. Form accountability pods of 3–5 people who check in weekly.

4. Run "Help Without Shame" campaigns for anonymous aid.

5. Establish a vision committee to shape long-term impact.

Small, steady steps build strong foundations. Grand speeches may inspire for a moment, but systems sustain for generations.

Examples of Community Turnarounds

In London, a once-dormant alumni group revived itself by setting a clear three-year vision: mentoring 100 students from their old school. They started with just ten mentors. Within a year, they had reached seventy-five. The group that used to argue over events was now united by purpose.

In Maryland, a small business forum introduced anonymous giving. Members could submit needs quietly, and others would respond privately. That system removed shame and restored dignity. People began to open up again.

In Germany, a multicultural professional network established "support trios" that checked in weekly. Each trio had one rule: no gossip, only growth. That single boundary kept relationships healthy and authentic.

Substance always attracts stability. Once a group becomes genuinely purposeful, people naturally want to stay.

Why Substance Requires Intentional Discomfort

Growth is uncomfortable. Accountability is inconvenient. Structure can feel restrictive. But without those, nothing meaningful lasts.

When a group begins to rebuild substance, it will face resistance. Some people will leave. Others will question motives. It is part of the process. Transformation always disturbs comfort zones.

True community is forged in friction, not flattery. The discomfort of being real is the price of being strong.

Rebuilding with substance means replacing performance with principles, activity with accountability, and events with impact. It means caring enough to ask the hard questions: Are we growing? Are we helping? Are we honest?

Substance will test your patience, but it will also secure your purpose.

And when your community finally finds its rhythm again, when people start checking on each other sincerely, when needs are met without shame, when purpose drives every plan, that is when the show ends and the real story begins.

Because it was never about looking like a family. It was about becoming one.

Reflection

And perhaps that is why some of us wake earlier than others — not because we are better, but because we are burdened to see.

Chapter 9: You're Not Crazy You're Just Awake

The Lonely Gift of Seeing Too Early

There is a strange ache that only visionaries understand. You see cracks forming long before the wall collapses, and when you speak up, everyone tells you to calm down. You sense decay beneath the noise of celebration, but they say you are overreacting. You try to realign a drifting group, and they call you difficult. Yet, when the crisis finally comes, they return, whispering, "You were right."

That is the price of being awake in a world that loves comfort.

Most communities, especially those built on tradition or hierarchy, struggle to handle people who see differently. They prefer predictability to progress. The phrase "Don't disturb a running process" has quietly become a shield against innovation. It sounds wise, but it is often just a way of protecting comfort zones.

In one of my alumni groups, I once began to raise concerns about the group's direction. I was not criticizing; I was caring. I spoke about purpose, inclusion, and growth. But the response was immediate discomfort. Leadership closed ranks. Messages were ignored. The familiar silence returned, that kind of silence so thick it could be cut with a knife.

In communities where hierarchy dominates, truth often becomes the first casualty. People confuse agreement with unity, so any form of questioning feels like rebellion. Yet genuine progress never comes from blind agreement; it comes from thoughtful confrontation.

The visionaries, the ones who dream of better structures, fairer systems, and deeper compassion, often find themselves isolated. They are not arrogant; they are just awake before the rest.

The Season of Loneliness

Being awake before others is not glamorous. It is often a season of silence, misunderstanding, and exhaustion. You watch people repeat mistakes you warned them about. You try to stay gracious, but your heart breaks when they call your honesty pride or bitterness.

I went through that cycle many times. In Cologne, during one community project, I tried to introduce a mentorship structure. I explained that the goal was sustainability, not control. But some people heard it differently. They thought I wanted attention. One even said, "Why are you trying to change what's already working?"

A year later, the group collapsed. The same people called to ask if I could help rebuild it. I said yes, but my heart was heavy. It was not satisfaction I felt; it was sorrow. Because I knew it didn't have to end that way.

Loneliness is the silent partner of vision. When you carry insight that others cannot yet see, you walk alone for a while. You doubt yourself. You replay conversations in your mind, wondering if you could have said it softer, slower, or smarter. But even if you did, it might not have changed anything. People awaken only when their season of comfort expires.

If you are the one who keeps noticing what others ignore, you are not crazy. You are simply called to see earlier.

The Sarcasm and the Subtle Silencing

Every visionary knows the sting of sarcasm. You share an idea, and someone smirks. You propose change, and someone jokes that you have too much time on your hands. They dismiss you with laughter because laughter is easier than listening.

It happens in churches, alumni groups, offices, even families. The one who suggests a new path threatens those who profit from the old one. So instead of open discussion, you get ridicule disguised as humor.

I once experienced this in Berlin during a planning meeting for a multicultural event. I suggested that we create a youth committee to help design the program. One man chuckled and said, "Ah, you like to complicate things." The room laughed. I smiled too, but inside, I felt that familiar fatigue, the exhaustion of being misunderstood on purpose.

Sarcasm is one of the quiet weapons of control. It tells you, "We hear you, but we won't change." It is the community's polite way of saying, "Stay in your lane."

Over time, that constant dismissal wears people down. The most talented minds retreat. The creative ones stop speaking. The reformers stop suggesting. Then the group begins to dry up, not because it lacked ideas, but because it suffocated the people who carried them.

The world loses countless innovations this way, not to ignorance, but to indifference.

When Talented People Leave

Every community that refuses to evolve eventually becomes a museum of memories. You will still have names, photos, and history, but the life will be gone.

Talented people do not leave because they are impatient; they leave because they are unacknowledged. They try to contribute, but the system resists them. Their ideas are ignored, their gifts uninvited, their potential misinterpreted. So they move on to spaces that value growth.

I have seen this happen across continents. In London, a talented designer left her cultural association after being told her ideas were "too modern." She went on to design campaigns for international organizations. When her old group saw her success online, they sent her congratulations, unaware that she had once begged for the chance to serve them.

In Maryland, a quiet accountant stopped attending her diaspora meetings because her suggestions about financial transparency were brushed aside. She later started a small accountability group that now funds scholarships for young migrants.

Every departure of a talented person is a warning bell that a culture is breaking. Communities that silence their thinkers eventually run out of ideas.

The Burden of Early Awareness

There were moments I thought something was wrong with me. Why did I always see things before they happened? Why did I feel urgency when others were still celebrating? Why did I speak up only to become the problem?

Then I realized: awareness is a gift, but it is also a burden. It keeps you awake while others sleep. It makes you restless while others relax. You begin to feel things before they surface. You speak things that later become headlines. It can be lonely, even painful, but it is also sacred.

In Germany, I used to notice patterns before they matured into crises, patterns of neglect, ego, or silence. I would mention them two years before they exploded. People often laughed or dismissed me. Then, two years later, they would say, "We wish we had listened earlier." That repeated experience taught me that timing is not always fairness.

The visionary's curse is to see what others can't yet handle. But your role is not to force them to see. Your role is to stay faithful to what you've been shown.

Encouragement for Builders, Not Just Attendees

If you are a builder in a world of attendees, do not apologize for your intensity. Your fire is not arrogance; it is assignment. Builders are the ones who turn gatherings into growth and noise into nourishment. They are not content with doing what has always been done. They ask the hard questions: "What is next? What can we improve? Who can we lift?"

Builders often look impatient because they see possibility everywhere. They see systems where others see comfort. They see opportunity where others see routine. But that same vision makes them misunderstood.

You may never get unanimous support, but you will find quiet allies, those who watch your courage and slowly begin to believe again. Leadership is often lonely at the start, but contagious over time.

If you have ever been told you are "too much," take heart. You are not too much; you are just early. You are not difficult; you are different. You are not crazy; you are awake.

How to Influence Change Without Burning Out

Change is beautiful, but it is also draining. The danger of being awake is that you can easily burn out from carrying too much vision for too long. The same sensitivity that helps you see ahead can also make you weary.

Here are a few lessons that have saved my sanity:

1. Stop trying to convince everyone.
Not everyone will understand your timing. Speak with wisdom, act with integrity, and let time be your evidence. Some lessons must unfold naturally.

2. Find a circle of fellow visionaries.
Every builder needs a space where their fire is understood. In Berlin, I found a small group of dreamers who met monthly just to share ideas and frustrations. We called it "Builders Anonymous." It became a lifeline.

3. Rest is part of revolution.
You cannot build what you do not replenish. Even God rested after creating. Take breaks. Reflect. Refill. Your vision deserves a healthy vessel.

4. Celebrate small wins.
Every change does not have to be massive to matter.

Sometimes your job is just to plant a seed. Growth will follow in its season.

5. Protect your heart from bitterness.
Nothing poisons a builder faster than resentment. Forgive quickly, release control, and remember why you began.

Being awake is not a curse. It is a calling. But every calling needs care.

The Beauty of Staying Awake

There will come a day when those who once resisted your voice will look back and see your intention clearly. Some will even thank you. But by then, you will have grown beyond needing their validation.

Being awake is not about proving you were right. It is about being faithful to truth, even when it costs comfort.

Visionaries are the early risers of humanity. They see dawn before others do. They stand by the window while the world still sleeps, whispering, "Morning is coming."

And when the light finally breaks, the same people who doubted them will step into that light, forgetting who lit the first candle. But the visionary smiles anyway, because their joy was never in recognition; it was in revelation.

So if you find yourself seeing deeper, feeling stronger, or thinking further than your circle, don't shrink. You're not crazy. You're just awake.

Stay awake. Stay kind. Stay building. The world still needs your voice.

Reflection

Awareness is not madness; it is the beginning of vision, and vision always demands building.

Chapter 10: Building What You Wish You Had

From Frustration to Foundation

Every visionary comes to a point where complaining no longer satisfies. You get tired of repeating what's broken. You get tired of seeing the same shallow patterns and hearing the same empty promises. There comes a day when your frustration transforms into focus. You stop asking, "Why doesn't someone fix this?" and you whisper, "Maybe I'm the one who's supposed to."

That moment is sacred. It is the bridge between awareness and action.

In every community, there are people quietly longing for what does not yet exist. A mentorship system that truly works. A platform that empowers without judgment. A network that listens without gossip. A safe space where vulnerability is not mistaken for weakness.

If you have ever wished such a place existed, then perhaps your wish is not random. It might be a calling. You are meant to build what you wish you had.

It does not have to begin grand. The strongest foundations are often laid in obscurity, in the quiet corners of chats and late-night thoughts, in small circles of genuine intent.

Starting Small but Strong

Change rarely begins with a crowd. It begins with conviction.

When you start something new, a group, an initiative, a mentorship space, it is tempting to wait until you have approval, funding, or a large audience. But history has shown that most lasting movements began with two or three committed people who believed something could be better.

I once joined a small circle of friends who wanted to support African youth studying abroad. We began with nothing but an idea, to connect students with mentors from different professions. We met at a café every Saturday morning, sharing laptops and tea. Within a year, we had matched forty students with mentors in various fields. The key was not size but sincerity.

In Germany, I watched a small church group evolve from Sunday fellowship to a social enterprise. They began by supporting one struggling mother with rent. That act inspired a ripple. Soon, they were helping others, creating job workshops, and raising tuition for young people.

Small beginnings are powerful because they force you to focus on essence. You learn what matters most. You learn how to sustain energy, not just excitement.

So if you feel led to start something, start small but strong. Choose structure over size. Choose purpose over publicity. Choose people who share your heart, not just your vision.

A Call to Action: Don't Wait for Permission

One of the greatest traps for visionary people is waiting for permission. Waiting for the right time. Waiting for approval from the right people. Waiting for consensus from those who may never understand your urgency.

You do not need everyone to agree before you move. You only need clarity of purpose and courage to begin.

When I first began writing publicly about the gaps in our communities, some people advised me to "wait until the atmosphere is right." Others said, "People are not ready for this kind of truth." But silence was suffocating me. The words would not stay contained. So I began. I wrote, I shared, and I built conversations that others were too polite to start.

Months later, those same people began to quote my words. They said, "This is exactly what we've been thinking." I smiled, not in pride but in gratitude. Because I learned that sometimes obedience must precede validation.

The world will not always announce your readiness. You must move even while uncertain, even when misunderstood.

Every great structure that exists today began as someone's small act of courage. The question is not whether you can change the world; it's whether you will change the corner of it that you touch.

Love, Faith, and Structure: The True Foundation of Community

Building anything meaningful requires more than passion. It requires love that forgives, faith that persists, and structure that sustains.

Love is the heart of every real community. It listens. It corrects gently. It gives without counting. It makes room for difference and still chooses unity. Without love, structure becomes control, and rules become walls instead of bridges.

Faith gives the builder endurance. Because in the early days, progress will be slow and appreciation scarce. Faith tells you that the seed will grow, even when the soil looks dry. Faith keeps you from giving up when you see no fruit yet.

Structure gives love direction and faith focus. It prevents burnout by creating systems that outlast emotion. Structure is why organizations thrive long after their founders step aside. It ensures that good intentions turn into consistent results.

A small women's business circle I once joined online began with spontaneous meetings and shared dreams. But without structure, they nearly fell apart after a few months. When they introduced roles, timelines, and accountability, everything changed. The same passion that once scattered them began to unite them. Love gave them purpose, faith gave them courage, but structure gave them sustainability.

A strong community is one that balances all three.

Planting Seeds for the Next Generation

Everything we build must point beyond us. If our success ends with us, it has failed its purpose.

The true measure of leadership is continuity. Can others continue what you started? Can your impact outlive your name?

In Cologne, I met a retired teacher who mentored young refugees. She told me something that stayed with me: "If you teach without preparing someone to take your place, you are building a monument, not a movement."

Her words carried truth. Too many groups die because no one was trained to continue the vision. The founder burns out, and the fire goes out with them. But when you empower others to lead, you plant seeds for generations.

Planting seeds means giving others a chance to learn, fail, and try again under your guidance. It means inviting younger voices to the table, not as guests but as partners. It means building systems that can evolve, not just repeat the past.

Mentorship is one of the most effective ways to plant such seeds. Every person who learns from you carries a piece of your vision forward.

Building what you wish you had means creating what others will one day thank you for. It is living with the awareness that your work is both present and prophetic.

The Ripple Effect

Every act of courage sets off ripples. You may never see the full impact of your effort, but it will travel farther than you imagine.

A word of encouragement can stop someone from giving up. A small job lead can change an entire family's trajectory. A mentorship call can ignite confidence in a young professional who thought they were invisible.

The beauty of building is that it multiplies unseen. You plant in faith, and somewhere, someone blooms in gratitude.

I have watched groups I once started grow beyond me. At first, it hurt to watch others take credit or lead in ways I might not have chosen. But then I realized that was the goal all along.

Builders are not owners; they are initiators. Once the structure stands, your joy is in seeing others thrive within it.

If your dream is pure, it will outgrow you.

You Are the Blueprint

Every time you think, "I wish there was a community that truly cared," the universe whispers back, "Then become that community."

You are the blueprint for what is missing. Your compassion, your restlessness, your ideas, they are not accidents. They are divine invitations to build.

So start small. Stay consistent. Lead with love. Anchor with faith. Protect with structure. And plant seeds so that long after you are gone, someone will look back and say, "Because of their courage, we now stand tall."

Building what you wish you had is not about changing the whole world. It is about shaping one corner of it so beautifully that others begin to believe again.

Because when one person decides to build with substance, hope finds a new address.

Reflection

And once we start building, we realize the silence was never empty — it was waiting for us to speak with substance.

Conclusion: Smiles Can Heal If They Come With Substance

When I began writing this book, I didn't know it would become both a confession and a mirror. A confession because I, too, have lived the quiet struggles I describe here. A mirror because as I wrote, I realized how many of us are trapped in the same story, smiling, showing up, posting, performing, but silently breaking inside.

The $200 Silence is not just a phrase; it is a symbol. It represents that small, invisible gap between help and hopelessness, between what we say and what we hide, between being seen and being truly known.

In truth, it is never just about money. The "$200" stands for those small acts of attention, empathy, and intervention that could change or even save a life. Sometimes all a person needs is someone to notice, to call, to listen, to lend a small hand before the silence swallows them whole.

We live in a world where people wait to express love at funerals and condolences replace conversations that should have happened long before. We have built communities that know how to celebrate but not how to sustain, how to take pictures but not how to notice pain.

This book is a call to awaken that lost sensitivity, to return to the kind of humanity that notices, that pauses, that acts.

What These Chapters Have Been Saying All Along

Every chapter in this book has been one piece of the same mosaic.

The Performance of Survival reminded us that pretending to be fine is exhausting and unsustainable. We wear smiles as armor, but every mask cracks eventually.

When Photos Replace Purpose exposed how social media and optics have replaced real connection. We learned that behind the most curated smiles are often unspoken struggles.

Death, Birthdays, and the Only Time People Speak showed us how easy it is to confuse digital engagement with care. We wake up for condolences and birthdays but sleep through one another's pain.

The Disappearing Ones made us face the tragedy of neglect, the people who fade away quietly while their communities stay busy posting. Some are gone before anyone notices.

When Mentorship Becomes Lifesaving reminded us that help does not always mean charity. It can be mentorship, a lead, an introduction, a reminder that someone still believes in you.

Unmasking the Culture of Performance pulled back the curtain on our obsession with status, showing that true value is not measured by how loud we appear but by how much we contribute to others.

The Crisis of No Structure explained why many good groups collapse, not from lack of love but lack of vision. Without clear direction, enthusiasm turns into exhaustion.

Rebuilding Community with Substance offered a blueprint for doing it right: defining shared purpose, establishing support systems, creating opportunities, and grounding everything in spiritual integrity.

You're Not Crazy You're Just Awake encouraged the builders, the early risers, the ones who see what others ignore, to stay faithful even when misunderstood.

And **Building What You Wish You Had** gave us the final push, the courage to start small, to act now, and to lead by example rather than waiting for approval.

Together, these chapters form one message: communities can heal when they return to substance.

Why This Book Exists

The $200 Silence exists for those who are tired of surface living. For the leaders who can no longer watch their people suffer behind smiles. For the young professionals searching for meaning in endless performance. For the builders who feel misunderstood for caring too much.

This book is for the mothers juggling bills in silence, for the fathers too proud to ask for help, for the alumni who want more than dinner pictures, for the believers who know faith must have hands.

It is a reminder that humanity still works. That we can still build groups that are not toxic or transactional. That we can laugh and still be honest. That love and structure can coexist.

It is also a challenge to stop waiting for others to fix the brokenness. We are the others. The responsibility to rebuild belongs to every one of us who sees the cracks.

A Handbook for Healing Communities

This book can be used as a handbook because it does not only expose what's wrong, it offers what's right. Every idea here can be applied in real life, in small, practical steps:

- **Listen intentionally.** Make space for someone's truth without rushing to fix it.

- **Create safety nets.** A small transition fund or mentorship directory can keep lives from unraveling.

- **Normalize checking in.** A five-minute call can ground someone standing on the edge.

- **Reward empathy as much as excellence.** Celebrate people for who they are, not just what they contribute.

- **Turn meetings into missions.** If your group gathers often, give each gathering purpose.

These are not theories. They are habits that can be practiced daily, in families, churches, alumni circles, workplaces, and neighborhoods.

This book invites us to move from talk to transformation.

Acknowledging Without Insecurity

Many groups struggle because acknowledgment has become a battlefield. Some feel threatened by another's growth, as if one person shining means another person fading. But acknowledgment is not competition; it is collaboration.

When you recognize someone else's strength, you expand the collective power of the group. When you allow others to lead, you teach humility by example. True leadership celebrates diversity of thought, talent, and calling.

We must outgrow the mindset that visibility equals superiority. Some of the best work happens in quiet rooms, through steady, unseen consistency. There is space for everyone's light when the room is built for growth, not comparison.

A healthy community knows how to celebrate without envy, correct without humiliation, and listen without defense. That is what substance looks like.

The Real Meaning of the $200 Silence

The "$200 Silence" is not only about money; it is about awareness. It is the space between noticing and acting, between saying "that's sad" and asking "how can I help?" It represents every moment we could have cared but didn't, every soul we could have checked on but forgot.

It also represents how small things can create large change. Sometimes it is literally a $200 gesture that saves a life. Other times, it is a kind message, a referral, a visit, a moment of empathy that reminds someone they matter.

The silence is deadly, not because people want to be ignored, but because we have normalized indifference. We call it respect, privacy, or "minding our business," but often it is fear or laziness. This book asks us to replace that silence with substance, to step into the quiet spaces where pain hides and bring light.

For the Builders and the Believers

This book belongs to the ones who have been misunderstood for caring too deeply. The ones who dream of communities that feel alive again. The ones who believe that love still works and that faith can rebuild what fear destroyed.

You are not asking for too much. You are simply remembering what being human feels like.

Keep building what you wish existed. Keep checking on those who fade. Keep showing up with intention. Keep believing that empathy is not weakness, that accountability is not attack, that structure is not control.

You are part of a quiet revolution, one where people choose depth over drama, purpose over popularity, and substance over show.

Smiles Can Heal If They Come With Substance

Celebration is not the problem. We can still have birthdays, photos, laughter, and events. Joy is necessary. But joy without awareness is denial.

So let us celebrate with compassion. Let our smiles be real, not rehearsed. Let our gatherings build bridges, not walls. Let our groups reflect purpose, not pretense.

Because smiles can heal, but only if they come with substance.

Let this book be more than a read. Let it be a reminder, a reference, a rebirth.

Because *The $200 Silence* is not just a story of lack. It is a story of possibility. It is proof that even in a world of noise, a single caring voice still matters.

And if we each decide to break that silence, not with noise, but with love, with structure, with faith, then maybe, just maybe, our communities will rise again.

Everyone Might be Smiling, But Nobody's Okay

References

1. The Gifts of Imperfection by Brené Brown

A groundbreaking book on embracing vulnerability, authenticity, and courage. Brené Brown encourages readers to let go of perfectionism and "who they think they should be" to embrace who they are.
Connection: This book mirrors the spirit of *The $200 Silence* by exposing the danger of performance-based living and the freedom in honest connection.

2. Daring Greatly by Brené Brown

A powerful exploration of vulnerability as a strength, not a weakness. Brown uses research to show how daring to be seen can transform relationships and leadership.
Connection: Resonates with the book's theme that real communities grow when people dare to be real, not perfect.

3. Leaders Eat Last by Simon Sinek

Sinek explains how great leaders create environments of trust and belonging where people feel safe and valued.
Connection: His insights on servant leadership align with the need for empathy and structure in rebuilding authentic communities.

4. The Art of Community by Charles Vogl

A practical guide on how communities form, thrive, and last. Vogl outlines timeless principles for creating belonging and shared purpose.
Connection: *The $200 Silence* draws from this idea that structure and shared vision are what give community its strength.

5. Bowling Alone: The Collapse and Revival of American Community by Robert D. Putnam

A sociological study on how modern society has lost its sense of community, leading to isolation and civic decline.
Connection: Offers data-backed evidence of the same disconnection and silence this book calls us to heal.

6. The Purpose Driven Life by Rick Warren

A Christian classic that focuses on living with divine purpose and serving others.
Connection: Deeply parallels the spiritual foundation of *The $200 Silence* in reminding readers that service, not status, defines meaningful living.

7. Man's Search for Meaning by Viktor E. Frankl

A timeless account of survival and purpose from the Holocaust, teaching that meaning is found through responsibility, not pleasure.

Connection: Echoes the book's message that purpose and compassion help people endure even when everything else fails.

8. The Emotionally Healthy Leader by Peter Scazzero

Scazzero explores how inner emotional health determines the integrity and longevity of leadership.
Connection: Relates directly to the chapter on leaders masking exhaustion with performance and the need for inner healing.

9. Everybody Always by Bob Goff

Bob Goff invites readers to love without limits and reach people where they are, not where we expect them to be.
Connection: Reflects the practical compassion and active empathy this book promotes love with hands and structure.

10. Atomic Habits by James Clear

Clear's book on how small, consistent actions create major transformations in life and systems.
Connection: Connects with *The $200 Silence's* teaching that small gestures, even $200 or a simple call, can transform lives.

11. The 7 Habits of Highly Effective People by Stephen R. Covey

Covey presents timeless principles of integrity, service, and proactive living.
Connection: Aligns with the book's call for responsibility, initiative, and structure in building thriving groups.

12. Find Your People by Jennie Allen

A contemporary Christian guide to building deep, authentic friendships in a disconnected world.
Connection: Strongly resonates with the book's focus on restoring trust, presence, and emotional honesty in modern relationships.

13. Quiet: The Power of Introverts in a World That Can't Stop Talking by Susan Cain

Cain celebrates introverts and the unseen power of quiet strength.
Connection: Complements *The $200 Silence's* understanding that silence is not always strength, but also that quiet presence, when intentional, can heal.

14. Community: The Structure of Belonging by Peter Block

Block presents a model for community transformation based on accountability, invitation, and shared ownership.

Connection: Mirrors the blueprint chapters of *The $200 Silence,* calling for purposeful gatherings over performative ones.

15. Start With Why by Simon Sinek

Sinek's powerful thesis that great movements and leaders inspire by communicating their "why" before their "what." **Connection:** Encourages communities to rediscover their purpose, the shared "why", before pursuing activities or appearances.

Action Appendix

Turning Awareness Into Action

Awareness is only powerful when it moves into action. These simple but intentional practices are how we turn empathy into structure and structure into hope.

1. **The $200 Mindset**

   Identify one small gesture each month that could relieve pressure for someone around you.

   Example: Cover a child's school lunch, fuel a single mother's car, buy groceries for a neighbor.

   It's not about the amount; it's about the awareness.

2. **The Check-In Challenge**

   Choose three people to check on monthly, not for business, but for life.

   Ask open questions like, "How's your energy this week?"

   Log their answers; consistency builds trust.

3. **Community Pulse Meetings**

   Encourage your group to hold quarterly "Pulse Gatherings."

   Instead of food or parties, make them 90-minute reflection sessions where people share real needs and wins.

4. **The Mentorship Chain**

   Pair professionals and students or those in transition.

   Keep sessions short but regular, a 30-minute monthly call can restore hope.

5. **The Vision Board for Groups**

   Every year, let the group co-create a purpose board:

   "What do we want to change?"

   "Whose life can we touch?"

   "Where can we grow?"

   This keeps structure alive and prevents stagnation.

6. **Help Without Shame Fund**

   A simple, transparent emergency fund managed by a small trusted committee.

   Members can request aid anonymously through a digital form.

   Reinforces that community help should carry dignity, not pity.

The $200 Silence ends when awareness becomes action, when empathy becomes habit, and when love finds a plan.

Author Bio

Rev. Dr. Ango Fomuso Ekellem is a global voice of wisdom, compassion, and faith whose work bridges spirituality, emotional intelligence, and practical humanity. With decades of experience in ministry, leadership, and cross-cultural service, she writes with the rare combination of depth, grace, and grounded truth that inspires both reflection and transformation.

Rooted in Africa, trained in Europe, and living in the United States, Rev. Fomuso Ekellem carries a global perspective shaped by years of ministry and mentorship across cultures. These experiences have deepened her understanding of resilience, migration, and the quiet battles people fight behind their smiles. Her ministry and writing flow from real encounters with individuals navigating hardship, transition, and hidden pain. Each experience has strengthened her commitment to restore dignity, empathy, and structure in human relationships.

The rare combination of an ordained chaplain, STEM and AI educator, university lecturer, and holder of an advanced degree in psychology gives Dr. Fomuso Ekellem a unique voice that blends science, faith, and the study of human behavior. Her teaching and mentorship unite critical thinking with compassion, showing how faith and intellect can work together to build stronger people and communities.

Her book, *The $200 Silence: Everyone's Smiling, But Nobody's Okay*, captures the heart of her mission. It is both a mirror and a manual, calling readers to unmask pretense, nurture community, and build systems of care that reach beyond words. Through stories drawn from everyday life, Rev. Dr. Ango Fomuso Ekellem reminds readers that awareness itself is a form of healing, and that sometimes, $200, a phone call, or a kind word can save a soul.

When she is not writing or mentoring, Rev. Fomuso Ekellem continues to build bridges across generations and continents. Her greatest joy is found in simple acts of connection, checking in, encouraging others, and proving that faith still has hands.